T0147915

Theory of Elastisity, Stability and Dynamics of Structures Common Problems

Konstantin Kazakov

ISBN: 978-1-4669-6862-2 (sc)
ISBN: 978-1-4669-6864-6 (hc)
ISBN: 978-1-4669-6863-9 (e)

Library of Congress Control Number: 2012922340

Trafford rev. 11/21/2012

 www.trafford.com

North America & international
toll-free: 1 888 232 4444 (USA & Canada)
phone: 250 383 6864 ♦ fax: 812 355 4082

Author: *Prof. Dr.Sc. Dr. Eng. Konstantin Kazakov*
Reviewer: *Assoc. Prof. Dr. Eng. Doncho Partov*

Contents

Preface

The content of the book is based on the lectures on the *Theory of Elasticity, Stability and Dynamics of structures.* The importance of these disciplines in the preparation of young structural engineers for work in the practice cannot be overemphasized. The university training in such fundamental discipline must seek to build a strong foundation and to illustrate the application of the used methods to practical engineering problems. The solution of a structural engineering problem usually consists of three basic steps: the simplification to such a state of idealization that it can be expressed in allegorical or geometrical form; the solution of this mathematical form; and the interpretation of the results of the solution in terms of the engineering needs. By successive illustration of these three steps in the solution of each problem the student must be lead and encourage approaching the solution of his own engineering problems in similar way or in similar manner with a desired degree of accuracy in the final result.

K. Kazakov

Chapter 1

Basic relations in Theory of elasticity

1.1 Theory of elasticity subject

The Theory of elasticity is engaged in research of the behavior of elastic bodies. A body is called *elastic* when it is capable of restoring its initial shape and dimensions, after the forces or reasons causing strains have been eliminated. A variety of materials could be assumed as elastic, up to a certain stress limits. That shows a presence of proportionality between strains and stresses. The relations between these quantities, i.e. strains and stresses, to the mentioned limits of stresses, are known as *Hooke's law* (Robert Hooke 1636-1703). In practice, the implemented proportionality is an idealization that leads to significant computational relieves.

1.2 Basic concepts and relations

In multitude of problems the atomic, discreet in nature, structure of the material can be ignored. The researched bodies are assumed to be continuous. In this way, the quantities are described by functions, defined as continuous in the body domain. This approach lies at the root of the Theory of elasticity.

Let us recall known from *Strength of materials* concepts, quantities, and their symbols (notations), in reference to one-dimensional problems.

Strains ε in one-dimensional are: the relation between the geometrical changes of dimension to the value of this dimension. They can be assumed as relative changes, and they are non-dimensional. They are related to stresses σ by material characteristics, called *modulus of elasticity*:

$$E = \frac{\sigma}{\varepsilon}. \qquad (i)$$

Another important material characteristic is *the Poisson's ratio*. It shows the relation between the strains, perpendicular to the direction of stresses and the parallel ones (parallel to the direction of stresses), i.e.:

$$\upsilon = \frac{\varepsilon_y}{\varepsilon_x} = \frac{\varepsilon_z}{\varepsilon_x}. \qquad (ii)$$

Besides the modulus of elasticity, we use modulus of shear strains:

$$G = \frac{\tau}{\gamma}. \qquad (iii)$$

The relation between the two modulii is:

$$G = \frac{E}{2(1+\upsilon)}. \qquad (iv)$$

Let us define three basic quantities, which are going to be used in Theory of elasticity, and to show the relations between them.

1.2.1 Displacement

When one body is subjected to certain effect, for instance, system of forces, then its points get displaced. *Displacements we call: the changes of the position of body's points, due to some effect (force) applied upon the body.* In the general case, the displacement can be expressed as a sum of two displacements—as an ideal rigid body displacement, and relative displacement of the points. Later on we are going to be interested only in relative displacements because they are the ones that caused strains and stresses.

Let us use one example, *Figure 1.1*. The body shown in the figure is supported in a way that displacements as an ideal rigid body are not possible, the body is restrained. Point *A* of the body Ω is shifted after loading, and its new position (location) is point $\bar{A}$, *Figure 1.1*.

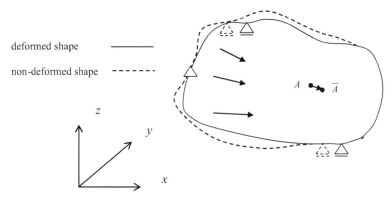

Figure 1.1.

The displacement at point can be expressed through its components in three orthogonal axes, for instance the Cartesian coordinate system $Oxyz$. These components are the projections of the displacement to corresponding axes, *Figure 1.2*. Then the vector, containing these values, scalars, can be written as:

$$\mathbf{U}(x,y,z) = \begin{Bmatrix} u(x,y,z) \\ v(x,y,z) \\ w(x,y,z) \end{Bmatrix}, \qquad (1.1)$$

where $u(x,y,z)$ is displacement in axis x, $v(x,y,z)$ - displacement in axis y, and $w(x,y,z)$ - displacement in axis z.

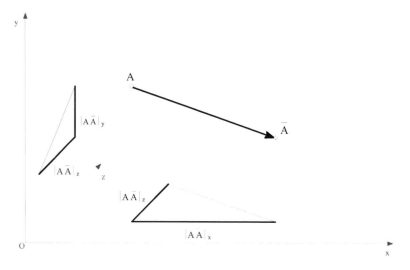

Figure 1.2.

1.2.2 Strain

When the distance between two points of the body changes, due to the loading, we assume that the body gets deformed. Strains can be expressed if the displacements are

4

known. Because of the body is treated as continuous, strains are continuous functions as well.

In the case of three-dimensional deformation, the vector of strains $\varepsilon(x, y, z)$ at point $A(x, y, z)$ of the body contains six components:

$$\varepsilon = \begin{Bmatrix} \varepsilon_x \\ \varepsilon_y \\ \varepsilon_z \\ \gamma_{xy} \\ \gamma_{yz} \\ \gamma_{zx} \end{Bmatrix}, \qquad (1.2)$$

where ε_x, ε_y and ε_z are linear strains in the coordinate axes, respectively x, y и z, and γ_{xy}, γ_{yz}, γ_{zx} are shear strains. They can be calculated by the relations:

$$\varepsilon_x = \frac{\partial u}{\partial x}, \qquad \varepsilon_y = \frac{\partial v}{\partial y}, \qquad \varepsilon_z = \frac{\partial w}{\partial z}$$

and

$$\gamma_{xy} = \frac{\partial u}{\partial y} + \frac{\partial v}{\partial x}, \quad \gamma_{yz} = \frac{\partial v}{\partial z} + \frac{\partial w}{\partial y}, \quad \gamma_{zx} = \frac{\partial w}{\partial x} + \frac{\partial u}{\partial z}. \qquad (1.3)$$

The deformations at a point are often shown in tensor form:

$$\mathbf{T}_\varepsilon = \begin{Vmatrix} \varepsilon_x & \dfrac{1}{2}\gamma_{yx} & \dfrac{1}{2}\gamma_{zx} \\ \dfrac{1}{2}\gamma_{xy} & \varepsilon_y & \dfrac{1}{2}\gamma_{zy} \\ \dfrac{1}{2}\gamma_{xz} & \dfrac{1}{2}\gamma_{yz} & \varepsilon_z \end{Vmatrix}. \qquad (1.4)$$

This tensor, and the stress tensor, which we are going to show below, both are symmetrical in regards to the leading diagonal. This means that for $\mathbf{T}_\varepsilon$ we have $\gamma_{yx} = \gamma_{xy}$, $\gamma_{zx} = \gamma_{xz}$ и $\gamma_{zy} = \gamma_{yz}$.

If we know the strains in three perpendicular directions, we are able to calculate the strain in arbitrary direction.

The strains in a body, or at a particular point of it, satisfy certain conditions, called *equations of continuity of the strains* or *compatibility conditions*. Thus, the equations of continuity of the strains appear as:

$$\frac{\partial^2 \varepsilon_x}{\partial y^2} + \frac{\partial^2 \varepsilon_y}{\partial x^2} = \frac{\partial^2 \gamma_{xy}}{\partial x \partial y};$$

$$\frac{\partial^2 \varepsilon_y}{\partial z^2} + \frac{\partial^2 \varepsilon_z}{\partial y^2} = \frac{\partial^2 \gamma_{yz}}{\partial y \partial z};$$

$$\frac{\partial^2 \varepsilon_z}{\partial x^2} + \frac{\partial^2 \varepsilon_x}{\partial z^2} = \frac{\partial^2 \gamma_{zx}}{\partial z \partial x};$$

$$2\frac{\partial^2 \varepsilon_x}{\partial y \partial z} = \frac{\partial}{\partial x}\left(-\frac{\partial \gamma_{yz}}{\partial x} + \frac{\partial \gamma_{zx}}{\partial y} + \frac{\partial \gamma_{xy}}{\partial z} \right);$$

$$2\frac{\partial^2 \varepsilon_y}{\partial z \partial x} = \frac{\partial}{\partial y}\left(\frac{\partial \gamma_{yz}}{\partial x} - \frac{\partial \gamma_{zx}}{\partial y} + \frac{\partial \gamma_{xy}}{\partial z} \right);$$

$$2\frac{\partial^2 \varepsilon_z}{\partial x \partial y} = \frac{\partial}{\partial z}\left(\frac{\partial \gamma_{yz}}{\partial x} + \frac{\partial \gamma_{zx}}{\partial y} - \frac{\partial \gamma_{xy}}{\partial z} \right). \tag{1.5}$$

We are going to show a proof of the first condition. Let us differentiate the forth equation in (1.3), i.e.:

$$\gamma_{xy} = \frac{\partial u}{\partial y} + \frac{\partial v}{\partial x} \qquad (1.6)$$

once in x and once in y. The result is:

$$\frac{\partial^2 \gamma_{xy}}{\partial x \partial y} = \frac{\partial^3 u}{\partial x \partial y^2} + \frac{\partial^3 v}{\partial x^2 \partial y}. \qquad (1.7)$$

Taking the consideration that

$$\frac{\partial^3 u}{\partial x \partial y^2} = \frac{\partial^2 \varepsilon_x}{\partial y^2} \quad \text{and} \quad \frac{\partial^3 v}{\partial x^2 \partial y} = \frac{\partial^2 \varepsilon_y}{\partial x^2}, \qquad (1.8)$$

we get:

$$\frac{\partial^2 \gamma_{xy}}{\partial x \partial y} = \frac{\partial^2 \varepsilon_x}{\partial y^2} + \frac{\partial^2 \varepsilon_y}{\partial x^2}. \qquad (1.9)$$

1.2.3 Stress

A certain field of strains corresponds to a certain field of stresses. At point $A(x, y, z)$ it has six components. Recorded as a vector, it appears as:

$$\sigma = \begin{Bmatrix} \sigma_x \\ \sigma_y \\ \sigma_z \\ \tau_{xy} \\ \tau_{yz} \\ \tau_{zx} \end{Bmatrix}, \qquad (1.10)$$

where σ_x, σ_y, σ_z are normal stresses, with directions in coordinate axes, respectively x, y and z, τ_{xy}, τ_{yz}, τ_{zx} are shear stresses. Under the notation τ_{xy} we are going to consider the shear stresses in a plane with a normal, parallel to axis x, acting in direction of axis y. The stresses are shown in *Figure 1.3.*

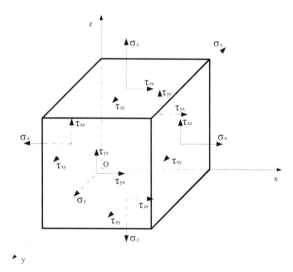

Figure 1.3.

The stresses at a point can be given in a tensor form as:

$$\mathbf{T_\sigma} = \begin{Vmatrix} \sigma_x & \tau_{yx} & \tau_{zx} \\ \tau_{xy} & \sigma_y & \tau_{zy} \\ \tau_{xz} & \tau_{yz} & \sigma_z \end{Vmatrix}. \tag{1.11}$$

Here $\tau_{yx} = \tau_{xy}$, $\tau_{zx} = \tau_{xz}$ and $\tau_{zy} = \tau_{yz}$. Each column of the tensor (1.11) corresponds to a plane with a normal, parallel to one of the coordinate axes x, y or z, i.e. gives the stresses, acting upon it. Each row, itself, shows the stresses in one of the directions.

1.2.4 Stress at a point in arbitrary (random) direction.

If the stresses in three perpendicular planes at point $A(x,y,z)$ are known, we can calculate the stress in a plane with arbitrary direction. Let us consider the tetrahedron, *Figure 1.4*. Its apex coincides with point $A(x,y,z)$, and has altitude h. The normal to the base is parallel to the direction of which we are interested the stress. Let us express it with n, and the stress with $\overline{p}^n$. The base area is denoted as F, and the directional cosines respectively as $\cos(n,x)$, $\cos(n,y)$ and $\cos(n,z)$.

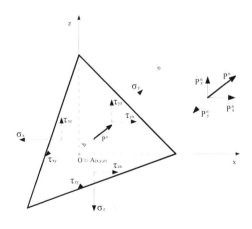

Figure 1.4.

9

The equation of equilibrium in x direction is:

$$\bar{p}_x^n F - \bar{\sigma}_x F \cos(n,x) - \bar{\tau}_{yx} F \cos(n,y) - \bar{\tau}_{zx} F \cos(n,z) + \frac{1}{3}FhP_x = 0,$$

(1.15)

where P_x are volume forces in x. If $h \to 0$, the forth term vanishes. Then, after dividing by F, we obtain:

$$p_x^n = \sigma_x \cos(n,x) + \tau_{yx} \cos(n,y) + \tau_{zx} \cos(n,z).$$ (1.16)

If $h \to 0$, stresses towards these at $A(x,y,z)$, i.e. $\bar{\sigma}_x \to \sigma_x$, $\bar{\tau}_{yx} \to \tau_{yx}$ and $\bar{\tau}_{zx} \to \tau_{zx}$.

Using the equations for equilibrium in y and z axes we obtain:

$$p_y^n = \tau_{xy} \cos(n,x) + \sigma_y \cos(n,y) + \tau_{zy} \cos(n,z)$$ (1.17)

and

$$p_z^n = \tau_{xz} \cos(n,x) + \tau_{yz} \cos(n,y) + \sigma_z \cos(n,z).$$ (1.18)

The stress p^n, acting at point $A(x,y,z)$, we calculate from:

$$\left| p^n \right| = \sqrt{\left(p_x^n\right)^2 + \left(p_y^n\right)^2 + \left(p_z^n\right)^2}.$$ (1.19)

1.2.5 Equations of equilibrium
Let us consider the elementary parallelepiped with sides dx, dy and dz, *Figure 1.5*. All of the stresses and volume forces, acting upon it are shown. In the figure, the stresses with differential increase are written below the wavy line, for instance $\tilde{\sigma}_x = \sigma_x + \dfrac{\partial \sigma_x}{\partial x} dx$.

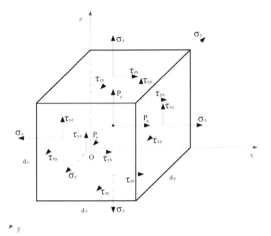

Figure 1.5.

Let us take only stresses, acting in coordinate direction x. Constituting the equation of equilibrium, we obtain:

$$\left(\sigma_x + \frac{\partial \sigma_x}{\partial x}dx - \sigma_x\right)dydz + \left(\tau_{yx} + \frac{\partial \tau_{yx}}{\partial y}dy - \tau_{yx}\right)dxdz +$$
$$+ \left(\tau_{zx} + \frac{\partial \tau_{zx}}{\partial z}dz - \tau_{zx}\right)dxdy + P_x dxdydz = 0 \qquad (1.20)$$

Relation (1.20) we divide by $dxdydz$. The result is:

$$\frac{\partial \sigma_x}{\partial x} + \frac{\partial \tau_{yx}}{\partial y} + \frac{\partial \tau_{zx}}{\partial z} + P_x = 0 \cdot \qquad (1.21)$$

By analogy, the equilibrium in other two coordinate directions leads to:

$$\frac{\partial \tau_{xy}}{\partial x} + \frac{\partial \sigma_y}{\partial y} + \frac{\partial \tau_{zy}}{\partial z} + P_y = 0 \qquad (1.22)$$

11

and

$$\frac{\partial \tau_{xz}}{\partial x} + \frac{\partial \tau_{yz}}{\partial y} + \frac{\partial \sigma_z}{\partial z} + P_z = 0 . \tag{1.23}$$

We will give a proof of the reciprocity of the shear stresses, for instance τ_{xz} and τ_{zx}, assuming that they refer to the centre of differential volume.

If we sum now the moments, related to axis y, we will get that:

$$\left(\tau_{zx} + \frac{\partial \tau_{zx}}{\partial z} \frac{dz}{2} \right) dxdy \frac{dz}{2} + \left(\tau_{zx} - \frac{\partial \tau_{zx}}{\partial z} \frac{dz}{2} \right) dxdy \frac{dz}{2} - \\ - \left(\tau_{xz} + \frac{\partial \tau_{xz}}{\partial z} \frac{dx}{2} \right) dydz \frac{dx}{2} - \left(\tau_{xz} - \frac{\partial \tau_{xz}}{\partial z} \frac{dx}{2} \right) dydz \frac{dx}{2} = 0 \tag{1.24}$$

or finally: $\tau_{zx} dxdydz = \tau_{xz} dxdydz$, i.e. $\tau_{zx} = \tau_{xz}$. Summation of moments towards axes x and z leads to $\tau_{yz} = \tau_{zy}$ and $\tau_{xy} = \tau_{yx}$, respectively.

1.2.6 Principal stresses

Through point $A(x, y, z)$ it is possible to draw three perpendicular planes, the stresses upon which correspond to the condition:

$$\sigma^3 - I_1 \sigma^2 - I_2 \sigma - I_3 = 0 , \tag{1.25}$$

where:

$$I_1 = \sigma_x + \sigma_y + \sigma_z , \tag{1.26}$$

$$I_2 = -\begin{vmatrix} \sigma_x & \tau_{yx} \\ \tau_{xy} & \sigma_y \end{vmatrix} - \begin{vmatrix} \sigma_x & \tau_{zx} \\ \tau_{xz} & \sigma_z \end{vmatrix} - \begin{vmatrix} \sigma_y & \tau_{zy} \\ \tau_{yz} & \sigma_z \end{vmatrix}, \qquad (1.27)$$

$$I_3 = -\begin{vmatrix} \sigma_x & \tau_{yx} & \tau_{zx} \\ \tau_{xy} & \sigma_y & \tau_{zy} \\ \tau_{xz} & \tau_{yz} & \sigma_z \end{vmatrix}. \qquad (1.28)$$

These planes are called *principal planes*, and the stresses *principal stresses*. We are going to denote these stresses as σ_1, σ_2 and σ_3. Typical for these planes is that, shear stresses are missing (zeros) upon them.

1.2.7 Relations between strains and stresses

There is a relation between strains and stresses. It is known as a general *Hooke's relation (Hooke's law)*. Can be written as:

$$\varepsilon_x = \frac{1}{E}\left[\sigma_x - \upsilon\left(\sigma_y + \sigma_z\right)\right];$$

$$\varepsilon_y = \frac{1}{E}\left[\sigma_y - \upsilon\left(\sigma_x + \sigma_z\right)\right];$$

$$\varepsilon_z = \frac{1}{E}\left[\sigma_z - \upsilon\left(\sigma_x + \sigma_y\right)\right];$$

$$\gamma_{xy} = \frac{2\left(1+\upsilon\right)}{E}\tau_{xy}; \quad \gamma_{yz} = \frac{2\left(1+\upsilon\right)}{E}\tau_{yz}; \quad \gamma_{zx} = \frac{2\left(1+\upsilon\right)}{E}\tau_{zx} \qquad (1.29)$$

and

$$\sigma_x = \frac{E}{(1+\upsilon)(1-2\upsilon)}\left[(1-\upsilon)\varepsilon_x + \upsilon\left(\varepsilon_y + \varepsilon_z\right)\right];$$

$$\sigma_y = \frac{E}{(1+\upsilon)(1-2\upsilon)}\left[(1-\upsilon)\varepsilon_y + \upsilon\left(\varepsilon_x + \varepsilon_z\right)\right];$$

$$\sigma_z = \frac{E}{(1+\upsilon)(1-2\upsilon)}\left[(1-\upsilon)\varepsilon_z + \upsilon\left(\varepsilon_x + \varepsilon_y\right)\right];$$

$$\tau_{xy} = \frac{E}{2(1+\upsilon)}\gamma_{xy}; \quad \tau_{yz} = \frac{E}{2(1+\upsilon)}\gamma_{yz}; \quad \tau_{zx} = \frac{E}{2(1+\upsilon)}\gamma_{zx}, \quad (1.30)$$

where E is a modulus of elasticity, and υ - Poisson's ratio.

It is completely obvious, from expressions (1.29) and (1.30) that, the relation between strains and stresses is linear, and depends on material constants. We could show it in a matrix form as:

$$\sigma = \begin{Bmatrix} \sigma_x \\ \sigma_y \\ \sigma_z \\ \tau_{xy} \\ \tau_{yz} \\ \tau_{zx} \end{Bmatrix} = \frac{E}{(1+\upsilon)(1-2\upsilon)} \begin{bmatrix} 1-\upsilon & \upsilon & \upsilon & 0 & 0 & 0 \\ \upsilon & 1-\upsilon & \upsilon & 0 & 0 & 0 \\ \upsilon & \upsilon & 1-\upsilon & 0 & 0 & 0 \\ 0 & 0 & 0 & \frac{1-2\upsilon}{2} & 0 & 0 \\ 0 & 0 & 0 & 0 & \frac{1-2\upsilon}{2} & 0 \\ 0 & 0 & 0 & 0 & 0 & \frac{1-2\upsilon}{2} \end{bmatrix} \begin{Bmatrix} \varepsilon_x \\ \varepsilon_y \\ \varepsilon_z \\ \gamma_{xy} \\ \gamma_{yz} \\ \gamma_{zx} \end{Bmatrix} .$$

$$(1.31)$$

1.3   Basic assumptions in Theory of elasticity

The basic assumptions, used in Theory of elasticity are:

- *Assumption for continuity of structures. We have already mentioned that, this precondition allows the use of functions, defined as continuous in the field (the domain) of the researched body. These functions describe the displacements, strains and stresses.*
- *The bodies are perfectly elastic. It means that, after removal of forces, they completely restore their dimensions and initial shape, i.e. the shape before the stress effect. This property is connected with proportionality of strains and stresses, i.e. the relation between these quantities is linear. The modulus of elasticity E is a constant, and in this case we are talking about material linearity.*
- *The effects upon bodies cause small displacements. It means that, the strains and the stresses can be described in the initial, non-deformed configuration of the bodies. When this assumption is not valid the mathematical model gets quite complicated. Then we are talking about large displacements, or about geometrical non-linearity.*
- *Saint-Venant's principle is valid.*

We are going to use the following additional assumptions:

- *The bodies are isotropic and homogeneous. This can be expressed as:* $E = E_x = E_y = E_z$.
- *The initial strains or stresses are zeros, i.e.* $\varepsilon_0 = 0$ *and* $\sigma_0 = 0$.

Chapter 2

Plane problems in Theory of elasticity

2.1. Theoretical summary of plane problems in Theory of elasticity

2.1.1 Equilibrium of plane rectangular differential element

The differential equilibrium equations, describing the plane problems in *Theory of elasticity* are derived from a plane rectangular differential element with sides dx and dy, *Figure 2.1*. This element is cut from a plane disk *1* m in thickness. The components of volume forces and the components of the stresses act along each side. For convenience the sides are assumed to be parallel to the coordinate axes. Obviously, the generalized forces act also in directions parallel to the coordinate axes.

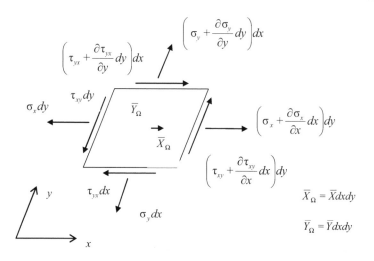

Fig. 2.1. Equilibrium of a plane rectangular differential element

If we consecutively constitute the following three equilibrium conditions $\sum X = 0$, $\sum Y = 0$ and $\sum M_P = 0$, where P coincides with the intersection point of the diagonals of the rectangular, we get:

$$\left(\sigma_x + \frac{\partial \sigma_x}{\partial x}dx\right)dy + \left(\tau_{yx} + \frac{\partial \tau_{yx}}{\partial y}dy\right)dx - \sigma_x dy - \tau_{yx}dx + \overline{X}dxdy = 0, \quad (2.1)$$

$$\left(\tau_{xy}dy + \left(\tau_{xy} + \frac{\partial \tau_{xy}}{\partial x}dx\right)dy\right)\frac{dx}{2} - \left(\tau_{yx}dx + \left(\tau_{yx} + \frac{\partial \tau_{yx}}{\partial y}dy\right)dx\right)\frac{dy}{2} = 0, \quad (2.2)$$

and

$$\left(\tau_{xy}dy + \left(\tau_{xy} + \frac{\partial \tau_{xy}}{\partial x}dx\right)dy\right)\frac{dx}{2} - \left(\tau_{yx}dx + \left(\tau_{yx} + \frac{\partial \tau_{yx}}{\partial y}dy\right)dx\right)\frac{dy}{2} = 0. \quad (2.3)$$

We would like to remind that in the *Mechanics*, the above mentioned conditions are called *First group conditions* of plane body equilibrium.

After arithmetical transformations and ignoring the infinitesimal members of higher order, can be written, respectively:

$$\frac{\partial \sigma_x}{\partial x} + \frac{\partial \tau_{yx}}{\partial y} + \overline{X} = 0, \tag{2.4}$$

$$\frac{\partial \tau_{xy}}{\partial x} + \frac{\partial \sigma_y}{\partial y} + \overline{Y} = 0 \qquad \text{and} \tag{2.5}$$

$$\tau_{xy} = \tau_{yx}. \tag{2.6}$$

Equations (2.4) and (2.5) express the conditions of the equilibrium of a plane rectangular differential element with sides dx and dy, and 2.6—the condition of reciprocity of shear stresses.

2.1.2 Boundary conditions

Boundary conditions, or also called contour conditions, could be expressed through the direct implementation of equilibrium equations of triangular differential element, with one of the sides lying onto the contour of plane area, i.e. plane disc. This side is its hypotenuse. This is illustrated in *Figure 2.2*.

It is important to emphasize that, the functions of the stresses have to be chosen in a way that the boundary conditions are satisfied for every particular problem, through this choice. It means that, the values of the functions of stresses over the disk's plane loaded contour, for instance, supposed to coincide with the intensity of the loading itself. If in this edge a loading is not present, then for its points the mentioned functions supposed to have zero values.

Let us express now the contour conditions, through the stresses σ_x, σ_y и τ_{xy}. Besides that, as we already mentioned, let the hypotenuse of the triangle, shown in *Figure 2.2.*, be a segment of the contour with a normal n, and length dn.

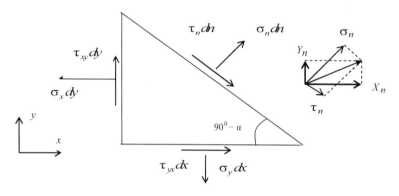

Figure 2.2. Equilibrium of a triangular differential element, bordering with the contour of the plane area

The equilibrium of the shown here triangular differential element in direction of the normal and the tangent towards the contour line is expressed as:

$$X_n = \sigma_x l + \tau_{yx} m \tag{2.7}$$

and

$$Y_n = \tau_{xy} l + \sigma_y m, \tag{2.8}$$

where l and m are the directional cosines of angle α or $l = \sin\alpha = dx / dn$ and $m = \cos\alpha = dy / dn$.

2.1.3   Relations between strains and displacements

The relations between strains and displacements are known also as *Cauchy relations*. They are expressed as:

$$\varepsilon_x(x,y) = \frac{\partial u(x,y)}{\partial x}, \qquad (2.9)$$

$$\varepsilon_y(x,y) = \frac{\partial v(x,y)}{\partial y} \qquad \text{and} \qquad (2.10)$$

$$\gamma_{xy} = \gamma_{yx} = \frac{\partial u(x,y)}{\partial y} + \frac{\partial v(x,y)}{\partial x}. \qquad (2.11)$$

If we differentiate eq. (2.9) two times to y, and eq. (2.10) two times to x, and add the left and the right sides (the right will be the mixed derivative of eq. (2.12)), we obtain the so-called *continuity condition of strains*. It is known also as *the Saint-Venant's condition*:

$$\frac{\partial^2 \varepsilon_x(x,y)}{\partial y^2} + \frac{\partial^2 \varepsilon_y(x,y)}{\partial x^2} = \frac{\partial^2 \gamma_{xy}(x,y)}{\partial x \partial y}. \qquad (2.12)$$

Since the expressions for displacements and strains are functions of both coordinates x and y, from a mathematical point of view eq. (2.12) represents a condition for continuity of the defined through (2.9), (2.10) and (2.11) functions in the disk's domain. In a case of linear behavior of the material, the strains correlate proportionally to the stresses.

From a physical point of view, the condition for continuity of the strains in researched body is a guarantee for its continuity.

2.1.4 Relations between stresses and strains

The expressions, characterizing the connection between stresses and strains are known as *generalized Hooke's relations*. These relations, related to plane problems, are shown below.

2.2 Plane stress and plane strain problems

2.2.1 Plane stress
- **Expressing the strains through stresses**

$$\varepsilon_x(x,y) = \frac{1}{E}\left(\sigma_x(x,y) - \upsilon\sigma_y(x,y)\right), \qquad (2.13)$$

$$\varepsilon_y(x,y) = \frac{1}{E}\left(\sigma_y(x,y) - \upsilon\sigma_x(x,y)\right), \qquad (2.14)$$

$$\gamma_{xy} = \gamma_{yx} = \frac{1}{G}\tau_{xy} = \frac{1}{G}\tau_{yx}, \qquad (2.15)$$

where E is modulus of elasticity, υ - Poisson's ratio, and G is modulus of shear strains, for which is valid that $G = \dfrac{E}{2(1+\upsilon)}$.

- **Expressing the stresses through strains**

$$\sigma_x(x,y) = \frac{E}{1-\upsilon^2}\left(\varepsilon_x(x,y) + \upsilon\varepsilon_y(x,y)\right), \qquad (2.16)$$

$$\sigma_y(x,y) = \frac{E}{1-\upsilon^2}\left(\varepsilon_y(x,y) + \upsilon\varepsilon_x(x,y)\right), \qquad (2.17)$$

$$\tau_{xy} = \tau_{yx} = G\gamma_{xy} = G\gamma_{yx}. \qquad (2.18)$$

2.2.2 Plane strain

- **Expressing the strains through stresses**

$$\varepsilon_x(x,y) = \frac{1}{\overline{E}}\left(\sigma_x(x,y) - \overline{\upsilon}\sigma_y(x,y)\right), \qquad (2.19)$$

$$\varepsilon_y(x,y) = \frac{1}{\overline{E}}\left(\sigma_y(x,y) - \overline{\upsilon}\sigma_x(x,y)\right), \qquad (2.20)$$

$$\gamma_{xy} = \gamma_{yx} = \frac{1}{\overline{G}}\tau_{xy} = \frac{1}{\overline{G}}\tau_{yx}, \qquad (2.21)$$

where

$$\overline{E} = \frac{E}{1-\upsilon^2},$$

$$\overline{\upsilon} = \frac{\upsilon}{1-\upsilon} \qquad \text{and}$$

$$\overline{G} = \frac{\overline{E}}{2(1+\overline{\upsilon})}. \qquad (2.22)$$

- **Expressing the stresses through strains**

$$\sigma_x(x,y) = \frac{\overline{E}}{1-\overline{\upsilon}^2}\left(\varepsilon_x(x,y) + \overline{\upsilon}\varepsilon_y(x,y)\right), \qquad (2.23)$$

23

Chapter **3**

Method of trigonometric series

3.1 Method of trigonometric series

The idea of method of trigonometric series is based on the use of *continuity of stresses equation* (the equation of Maurice Levy), where the functions of normal and tangential stresses are expressed through auxiliary function, called function of *Airy*. This function could be represented through infinite trigonometric series. The usage of infinite trigonometric series in the functions of stresses, and from there, in the function of loading (as boundary values of stresses) allows them to get expressed through a sum of infinite amount of trigonometric terms. This sum can be limited, because the contribution of every next term decreases greatly. This is predetermined by the type of coefficients, which we are going to call *weights*.

At the beginning we will recall things, known from the previous chapter. Let us use the differential equilibrium eqs. (2.4) and (2.5), and the continuity of strains condition as well eq. (2.12) expressed here again:

$$\frac{\partial \sigma_x}{\partial x} + \frac{\partial \tau_{yx}}{\partial y} + \overline{X} = 0, \tag{3.1}$$

$$\frac{\partial \tau_{xy}}{\partial x} + \frac{\partial \sigma_y}{\partial y} + \overline{Y} = 0 \qquad \text{and} \tag{3.2}$$

$$\frac{\partial^2 \varepsilon_x (x, y)}{\partial y^2} + \frac{\partial^2 \varepsilon_y (x, y)}{\partial x^2} = \frac{\partial^2 \gamma_{xy} (x, y)}{\partial x \partial y}. \tag{3.3}$$

If the components of volume forces are assumed to be constant, then using eqs. (2.13), (2.14) and (2.15) substituted in (3.3), and expressing the shear stresses through the normal stresses, where we use eq. (3.1) differentiated to x, and eq. (3.2) to y, we obtain:

$$\frac{\partial^2 \sigma_x}{\partial x^2} + \frac{\partial^2 \sigma_y}{\partial x^2} + \frac{\partial^2 \sigma_x}{\partial y^2} + \frac{\partial^2 \sigma_y}{\partial y^2} = 0. \tag{3.4}$$

This relation is known as *equation of Maurice Levy*, or *equation for continuity of stresses*. It could be expressed in the form:

$$\left(\frac{\partial^2}{\partial x^2} + \frac{\partial^2}{\partial y^2} \right) \left(\sigma_x + \sigma_y \right) = \nabla^2 \left(\sigma_x + \sigma_y \right) = 0, \tag{3.5}$$

where ∇^2 is *Laplace operator.*

If we use the differential equilibrium eqs. (3.1) and (3.2), together with the equation of Maurice Levy (3.4), we could find the functions of stresses $\sigma_x (x, y)$, $\sigma_y (x, y)$ and $\tau_{xy} (x, y)$ in the disk's domain, in given boundary conditions.

We are going to express the functions of stresses $\sigma_x (x, y)$, $\sigma_y (x, y)$ and $\tau_{xy} (x, y)$ through the auxiliary function $\varphi(x, y)$, called function of *Airy*, defined as continuous in the same domain.

Assuming the volume forces are constants, we introduce the expressions:

$$\sigma_x\left(x,y\right)=\frac{\partial^2\varphi\left(x,y\right)}{\partial y^2}-\overline{X}.x\,, \tag{3.6}$$

$$\sigma_y\left(x,y\right)=\frac{\partial^2\varphi\left(x,y\right)}{\partial x^2}-\overline{Y}.y \qquad \text{and} \tag{3.7}$$

$$\tau_{xy}\left(x,y\right)=-\frac{\partial^2\varphi\left(x,y\right)}{\partial x\partial y}. \tag{3.8}$$

When we substitute eqs. (3.6), (3.7) and (3.8) in eqs. (3.1) and (3.2), we get identities:

$$\frac{\partial}{\partial x}\left(\frac{\partial^2\varphi\left(x,y\right)}{\partial y^2}\right)+\frac{\partial}{\partial y}\left(-\frac{\partial^2\varphi\left(x,y\right)}{\partial x\partial y}\right)+\overline{X}-\overline{X}=0 \tag{3.9}$$

and

$$\frac{\partial}{\partial x}\left(-\frac{\partial^2\varphi\left(x,y\right)}{\partial x\partial y}\right)+\frac{\partial}{\partial y}\left(\frac{\partial^2\varphi\left(x,y\right)}{\partial x^2}\right)+\overline{Y}-\overline{Y}=0\,. \tag{3.10}$$

Repeating the same operation in eq. (3.4), we get:

$$\left(\frac{\partial^2}{\partial x^2}+\frac{\partial^2}{\partial y^2}\right)\left(\frac{\partial^2\varphi\left(x,y\right)}{\partial y^2}-\overline{X}.x+\frac{\partial^2\varphi\left(x,y\right)}{\partial x^2}-\overline{Y}.y\right)=0 \tag{3.11}$$

or

$$\frac{\partial^4}{\partial x^4}\varphi\left(x,y\right)+2\frac{\partial^4}{\partial x^2\partial y^2}\varphi\left(x,y\right)+\frac{\partial^4}{\partial y^4}\varphi\left(x,y\right)=0\,. \tag{3.12}$$

27

Equation (3.12) is symbolically expressed through the differential Laplace's operator as:

$$\nabla^2\nabla^2\varphi(x,y)=\nabla^4\varphi(x,y)=0.$$ (3.13)

In the last stage of the method, the auxiliary function of Airy is expressed as infinite single or double trigonometric series, depending on the loading.

In this case, i.e. in rectangular domain, rectangular wall, supported in the vertical edges by mechanisms, absorbing the shear stresses, and load on the upper edge, the function of Airy could be used in this form:

$$\varphi(x,y)=\sum_{i=1}^{\infty}Y_i(y)\sin\frac{i\pi}{l}x.$$ (3.14)

Relation (3.14), consists products of harmonic ($\sin\frac{i\pi}{l}x$) and weight ($Y_i(y)$) functions. The second ones are greatly decrease with i increase. In practice only limited numbers of terms give acceptable results.

The algorithm of the solution consists of following steps:

1. *Expressing the stresses* $\sigma_x(x,y)$, $\sigma_y(x,y)$ *and* $\tau_{xy}(x,y)$ *by auxiliary function, say (3.14).*
2. *Defining function* $Y_i(y)$, *used in (3.14) by the boundary conditions.*
3. *Expressing the general integral of the bi-harmonical equation, expressed as (3.12) or (3.13), in hyperbolo-trigonometric series.*
4. *Defining its coefficients by the boundary conditions.*
5. *Final form of the functions of stresses.*
6. *Verifications.*

We are going to follow these steps, and demonstrate them. Let us examine a rectangular disk, with measures l and h respectively, 1m in thick. The disk is loaded on the upper edge, i.e. line $l^{up}(x,h)$ and is supported by mechanisms, absorbing only the shear stresses. This setting is illustrated in *Figure3.1.*

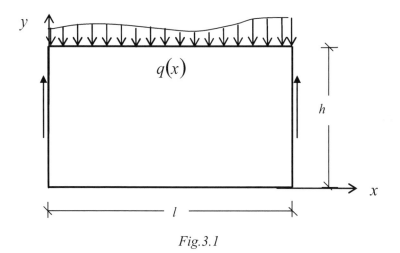

Fig.3.1

3.1.1 Expressing of the stresses $\sigma_x(x,y)$, $\sigma_y(x,y)$ and $\tau_{xy}(x,y)$

This step is expressed through eqs. (3.6), (3.7) and (3.8). Let us substitute eq. (3.14) in (3.6), (3.7) and (3.8). The result is:

$$\sigma_x(x,y)=\frac{\partial^2\varphi(x,y)}{\partial y^2}=\sum_{i=1}^{\infty}Y_i^{''}(y)\sin\frac{i\pi}{l}x,\qquad(3.15)$$

$$\sigma_y(x,y)=\frac{\partial^2\varphi(x,y)}{\partial x^2}=-\sum_{i=1}^{\infty}\left(\frac{i\pi}{l}\right)^2 Y_i(y)\sin\frac{i\pi}{l}x\quad\text{and}\quad(3.16)$$

29

$$\tau_{xy}\left(x,y\right)=-\frac{\partial^2\varphi\left(x,y\right)}{\partial x \partial y}=-\sum_{i=1}^{\infty}\frac{i\pi}{l}Y_i^{'}\left(y\right)\cos\frac{i\pi}{l}x. \qquad (3.17)$$

Let us substitute now eq. (3.14) in (3.11) or (3.12), we get:

$$\sum_{i=1}^{\infty}\left(Y_i^{IV}\left(y\right)-2\left(\frac{i\pi}{l}\right)^2 Y_i^{''}\left(y\right)+\left(\frac{i\pi}{l}\right)^4 Y_i\left(y\right)\right)\sin\frac{i\pi}{l}x=0. \quad (3.18)$$

This could be satisfied for every x, if:

$$Y_i^{IV}\left(y\right)-2\left(\frac{i\pi}{l}\right)^2 Y_i^{''}\left(y\right)+\left(\frac{i\pi}{l}\right)^4 Y_i\left(y\right)=0. \qquad (3.19)$$

The eq. (3.19) is fourth order deferential equation with constant coefficients.

3.1.2 Defining of $Y_i\left(y\right)$ and expressing the boundary conditions

The function $Y_i\left(y\right)$ supposed to be chosen from such a type, in terms to become a solution of (3.19), and at the same time to ensure the distribution of stresses in coordinate direction y, corresponding to the conditions in the boundaries. These boundaries, in this case, are: the upper and the lower edge of the disk. A function, satisfying these requirements, is expressed as:

$$Y_i\left(y\right)=A_i ch\alpha_i y+B_i sh\alpha_i y+C_i ych\alpha_i y+D_i ysh\alpha_i y, \qquad (3.20)$$

where: $\alpha_i = \dfrac{i\pi}{l}$. The coefficients are defined by the boundary conditions. In this case, rectangular domain, the conditions can be expressed as:

- $\sigma_y(x,0)=0$

The stresses σ_y on the lower edge are zeros, i.e.:

$$\sigma_y(x,0)=\frac{\partial^2\varphi(x,0)}{\partial x^2}=-\sum_{i=1}^{\infty}\alpha_i^2 Y_i(0)\sin\alpha_i x=0,\qquad(3.21)$$

which is satisfied if $Y_i(0)=0$, i.e. $A_i=0$.

- $\tau_{xy}(x,0)=0$

The stresses τ_{xy} on the lower edge are zeros. We express as:

$$\tau_{xy}(x,0)=-\frac{\partial^2\varphi(x,0)}{\partial x\partial y}=-\sum_{i=1}^{\infty}\alpha_i Y_i'(0)\cos\alpha_i x=0,\qquad(3.22)$$

which is satisfied if $Y_i'(0)=0$.

- $\tau_{xy}(x,h)=0$

The stresses τ_{xy} on the upper edge of the disk are also zeros. i.e.:

$$\tau_{xy}(x,h)=-\frac{\partial^2\varphi(x,h)}{\partial x\partial y}=-\sum_{i=1}^{\infty}\alpha_i Y_i'(h)\cos\alpha_i x=0,\qquad(3.23)$$

which is satisfied if $Y_i'(h) = 0$.

- $\sigma_y(x,h) = -q(x)$

The stresses σ_y on the upper edge supposed to be equal to the loading, admitted with an opposite sign. This represents, so-called in Chapter 2. boundary condition in loading contour. We have:

$$\sigma_y(x,h) = \frac{\partial^2 \varphi(x,h)}{\partial x^2} = -\sum_{i=1}^{\infty} \alpha_i^2 Y_i(h)\sin \alpha_i x = -q(x). \quad (3.24)$$

We substitute $\alpha_i^2 Y_i(h) = q_i$ and get:

$$\sum_{i=1}^{\infty} q_i \sin \alpha_i x = q(x). \qquad (3.25)$$

Condition (3.25) has been satisfied, because it represents a quotient case of Discrete Fourier transformation. We will prove that. Let us multiply both sides of eq. (3.25) by the trigonometric multiplier $\sin \alpha_i x$ and let integrate on the length of the upper edge. We get:

$$\sum_{\bar{i}=1}^{\infty} q_{\bar{i}} \sin \alpha_{\bar{i}} x \sin \alpha_i x = q(x)\sin \alpha_i x \qquad (3.26)$$

and

$$\sum_{\bar{i}=1}^{\infty} q_{\bar{i}} \int_0^l \sin \alpha_{\bar{i}} x \sin \alpha_i x dx = \int_0^l q(x)\sin \alpha_i x dx. \qquad (3.27)$$

From the infinite sum in the left side of eq. (3.27) there is only one addend remaining. This is the addend, corresponding to the right side index (to the index of the trigonometric multiplier, i.e. $\bar{i} = i$). This fact is a result of the property orthogonality of trigonometric functions, when i are positive numbers. Performing the integration, we will get:

$$q_i \int_0^l \sin^2 \alpha_i x dx = q_i \frac{l}{2}. \qquad (3.28)$$

This result, substituted in eq. (3.27), leads to:

$$q_i \frac{l}{2} = \int_0^l q(x) \sin \alpha_i x dx \qquad (3.29)$$

or

$$q_i = \frac{2}{l} \int_0^l q(x) \sin \alpha_i x dx. \qquad (3.30)$$

The couple of expressions (3.25) and (3.30) represent the forward and inverse transformation of functions q_i and $q(x)$. Similar transformation will be used in *Chapter 5*, when introducing the *Method of Navier.*

Let us get back to the condition (3.25), where it was replaced with $\alpha_i^2 Y_i(h) = q_i$. The same replacement we could write as:

$$Y_i(h) = \frac{q_i}{\alpha_i^2}. \qquad (3.31)$$

33

3.1.3 Finding of the general integral of the bi-harmonical eqs. (3.12) or (3.13)

We have said that the integral of eq. (3.19) we are searching for in the form (3.20). After being obtained, the integral of (3.19) is replaced in (3.14), and in this way the auxiliary function satisfies: the equilibrium relations, the continuity equation and the boundary conditions. We will mention again that, for the latest to be present, i.e. the boundary conditions, it is necessary the coefficients A_i, B_i, C_i and D_i to be obtained in such a way that eqs. (3.21), (3.22), (3.23) and (3.24) have been satisfied.

3.1.4 Defining of A_i, B_i, C_i and D_i through the boundary conditions.

The coefficients A_i, B_i, C_i and D_i, defined in a way that eqs. (3.21), (3.22), (3.23) and (3.24) have been satisfied, are expressed as:

$$A_i = 0, \tag{3.32}$$

$$B_i = -\frac{q_i}{\alpha_i^2}\frac{\sinh\alpha_i h + \alpha_i h.\cosh\alpha_i h}{\left(\alpha_i h\right)^2 - \sinh^2\alpha_i h}, \tag{3.33}$$

$$C_i = \frac{q_i}{\alpha_i}\frac{\sinh\alpha_i h + \alpha_i h.\cosh\alpha_i h}{\left(\alpha_i h\right)^2 - \sinh^2\alpha_i h}, \tag{3.34}$$

$$D_i = -\frac{q_i}{\alpha_i}\frac{\alpha_i h.\sinh\alpha_i h}{\left(\alpha_i h\right)^2 - \sinh^2\alpha_i h}. \tag{3.35}$$

3.1.5 Final form of the functions of the stresses.

If we assume the expressions:

$$B_i = \bar{B}_i\frac{q_i}{\alpha_i^2}, \; C_i = \bar{C}_i\frac{q_i}{\alpha_i}, \; D_i = \bar{D}_i\frac{q_i}{\alpha_i} \tag{3.36}$$

and substitute them in eq. (3.14), and, through that, also in eqs. (3.15), (3.16) and (3.17) we get:

$$\sigma_x = \sum_{i=1}^{\infty}\left[-\bar{B}_i\left(\sinh\alpha_i y + \alpha_i y.\cosh\alpha_i y\right)+\bar{D}_i\left(2\cosh\alpha_i y+\alpha_i y.\sinh\alpha_i y\right)\right]q_i\sin\alpha_i x$$
(3.37)

$$\sigma_y = -\sum_{i=1}^{\infty}\left[\bar{B}_i\left(\sinh\alpha_i y - \alpha_i y.\cosh\alpha_i y\right)+\bar{D}_i\alpha_i y.\sinh\alpha_i y\right]q_i\sin\alpha_i x,$$
(3.38)

$$\tau_{xy} = \tau_{yx} = -\sum_{i=1}^{\infty}\left[-\bar{B}_i\alpha_i y.\sinh\alpha_i y+\bar{D}_i\left(\sinh\alpha_i y+\alpha_i y.\cosh\alpha_i y\right)\right]q_i\sin\alpha_i x$$
(3.39)

using that $\bar{B}_i = -\bar{C}_i$.

The calculating procedure, from now on, is based on the introduction of the coordinates of specific point, and the calculation of terms. For instance, if we are interested in the stress σ_x, we calculate σ_x^1, σ_x^2, σ_x^3, σ_x^4, σ_x^5 ... etc. Because of $\bar{B}_i$ and $\bar{D}_i$ are greatly decrease in value functions, this allows limited number terms to be calculated.

Based on eqs. (3.37), (3.38) and (3.39) we could make the following conclusion. The stresses at a point are obtained as a superposition of the contributions of every term from the decomposition of the load, type $q_i\sin\alpha_i x$. It means that, every addend σ_x^i is a stress, obtained from load $q_i\sin\alpha_i x$.

3.2. Verifications

The calculations, conducted by the Method of trigonometric series, could be verified through different simplified methods, or through *The Finite Element Method (FEM)*.

Chapter 4

Theories for bending of thin and moderate thick elastic plates

4.1   Review of the theories for bending of elastic plates

There are several theories for bending of smooth elastic plates. The main differences between them are in the assumptions, used for obtaining the principal relations. These assumptions define the so-called accuracy of the model of bending. In other words, this is the authenticity of mathematical model, in terms of the actual behavior. The above mentioned mathematical model is an inseparable part of the whole computational model. The most important of the assumptions is the one, related to the deformation of the cross section.

4.2   Theory of Kirchhoff

Because of the simplicity the theory for bending of smooth thin elastic plates, or known as *theory of Kirchhoff*, is probably the most applied plate theory. The above mentioned simplicity is based on its assumptions. This theory is often called *engineering* or *classical theory* for bending of smooth thin elastic plates. From now on we are going to skip the term smooth, but we are going to assume that.

In the theory of Kirchhoff the following assumptions are used:

- *After applying the loading, the points in the middle plane of the plate are getting displaced only in the direction of axis z.*

Certain expressions are valid about the displacements of the middle plane of the plate:

$$u\left(x, y, z_0\right) = u_0 = 0,$$

$$v\left(x, y, z_0\right) = v_0 = 0, \qquad (4.1.a)$$

$$w\left(x, y, z_0\right) = w_0 \neq 0,$$

where the lower index 0 is used, to show that the points are located upon the middle plane of the plate before loading. If the coordinate system is positioned in the way, shown in *Figure 4.1*, the expressions (4.1.a) we could write as:

$$u\left(x, y, 0\right) = u_0 = 0,$$

$$v\left(x, y, 0\right) = v_0 = 0, \qquad (4.1.b)$$

$$w\left(x, y, 0\right) = w_0 \neq 0.$$

- *Every segment with length h, perpendicular to the middle plane of the plate before the loading keeps its length and remains perpendicular to the tangent towards the middle surface after the loading.*

The above assumption with the first one can be expressed as:

$$w(x, y, z_0) = w(x, y, 0) = w_0 \neq 0$$

and

$$\gamma_{xz} = \gamma_{yz} = 0. \tag{4.2}$$

- *The normal stresses σ_z are insignificant and can be ignored.*

This can be expressed as:

$$\varepsilon_z = 0. \tag{4.3}$$

If we consider the above preconditions, and examine the position of point A from the vertical cross section, at a distance z from the middle plane before the loading *(see Figure 4.1)*, we could write the following:

$$u(x, y, z) = -z \sin \alpha \approx -z tg\alpha = -z \frac{\partial w}{\partial x}, \tag{4.4}$$

$$v(x, y, z) = -z \frac{\partial w}{\partial y}, \tag{4.5}$$

$$w(x, y, z) = w(x, y, 0) = w_0. \tag{4.6}$$

We can see that the vertical (transverse) displacements of the points is function only of the coordinates x and y. The first partial derivatives of the displacements coincide with the rotations of the cross section, i.e. $\dfrac{\partial w(x, y)}{\partial x} \equiv \varphi_y(x, y)$ and $\dfrac{\partial w(x, y)}{\partial y} \equiv \varphi_x(x, y)$. If they are known, the horizontal displacements of whichever point we could find after multiplying these rotations by the coordinate z, measured from the middle plane. The lower index in the left side of the expressions shows the direction of the vector of rotation.

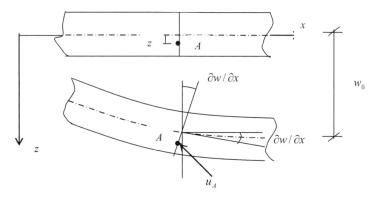

Figure 4.1: Deformation of thin elastic plate

Everything said so far is valid if displacements are small. In this case we could assume that $\sin \alpha \approx tg\alpha$.

The strains at the point can be expressed as:

$$\varepsilon_x = \frac{\partial}{\partial x} u\left(x, y, z\right) = -z \frac{\partial^2 w\left(x, y\right)}{\partial x^2}, \tag{4.7}$$

$$\varepsilon_y = \frac{\partial}{\partial y} v\left(x, y, z\right) = -z \frac{\partial^2 w\left(x, y\right)}{\partial y^2}, \tag{4.8}$$

and

$$\gamma_{xy} = \frac{\partial}{\partial y} u\left(x, y, z\right) + \frac{\partial}{\partial x} v\left(x, y, z\right) = -2z \frac{\partial^2 w\left(x, y\right)}{\partial x \partial y}. \tag{4.9}$$

The material is linearly elastic and the stresses are derived from the *Hooke's law.* They are written as:

$$\sigma_x = \frac{E}{1-\upsilon^2}\left(\varepsilon_x + \upsilon\varepsilon_y\right) = -\frac{Ez}{1-\upsilon^2}\left(\frac{\partial^2 w}{\partial x^2} + \upsilon\frac{\partial^2 w}{\partial y^2}\right), \qquad (4.10.a)$$

$$\sigma_y = \frac{E}{1-\upsilon^2}\left(\varepsilon_y + \upsilon\varepsilon_x\right) = -\frac{Ez}{1-\upsilon^2}\left(\frac{\partial^2 w}{\partial y^2} + \upsilon\frac{\partial^2 w}{\partial x^2}\right), \qquad (4.11.a)$$

$$\tau_{xy} = \tau_{yx} = G\gamma_{xy} = G\gamma_{yx} = -\frac{Ez}{1+\upsilon}\frac{\partial^2 w}{\partial x\partial y}. \qquad (4.12.a)$$

The second partial derivatives in the above relations represent the curvatures of bending and torsion for a point of the middle plane. Because of that the above relations, we could write that:

$$\sigma_x = -\frac{Ez}{1-\upsilon^2}\left(\chi_x + \upsilon\chi_y\right), \qquad (4.10.b)$$

$$\sigma_y = -\frac{Ez}{1-\upsilon^2}\left(\chi_y + \upsilon\chi_x\right), \qquad (4.11.b)$$

$$\tau_{xy} = \tau_{yx} = G\gamma_{xy} = G\gamma_{yx} = -\frac{Ez}{1+\upsilon}\chi_{xy}, \qquad (4.12.b)$$

where: $\chi_x = \dfrac{1}{\rho_x} = \dfrac{\partial^2 w}{\partial x^2}$, $\chi_y = \dfrac{1}{\rho_y} = \dfrac{\partial^2 w}{\partial y^2}$ and $\chi_{xy} = \dfrac{1}{\rho_{xy}} = \dfrac{\partial^2 w}{\partial x\partial y}$.

Here with ρ are expressed the radii of a curvature.

The expressions for bending and torsional moments M_x, M_y, M_{xy} and for the shear forces Q_x and Q_y look like:

$$M_x = \int_{-h/2}^{h/2} z\sigma_x dz = -D\left(\frac{\partial^2 w}{\partial x^2} + \upsilon\frac{\partial^2 w}{\partial y^2}\right), \qquad (4.13)$$

$$M_y = \int_{-h/2}^{h/2} z\sigma_y dz = -D\left(\frac{\partial^2 w}{\partial y^2} + \upsilon\frac{\partial^2 w}{\partial x^2}\right), \qquad (4.14)$$

$$M_{xy} = \int_{-h/2}^{h/2} z\tau_{xy} dz = -D(1-\upsilon)\frac{\partial^2 w}{\partial x\partial y} \qquad (4.15)$$

and

$$Q_x = \int_{-h/2}^{h/2} \tau_{xz} dz = -D\frac{\partial}{\partial x}\nabla^2 w, \qquad (4.16)$$

$$Q_y = \int_{-h/2}^{h/2} \tau_{yz} dz = -D\frac{\partial}{\partial y}\nabla^2 w, \qquad (4.17)$$

where:

$$D = \frac{Eh^3}{12(1-\upsilon^2)} \qquad (4.18)$$

is called *cylindrical* or *plate stiffness*. Here E is a modulus of elasticity, and υ - Poisson's ratio. In eqs. (4.16) and (4.17) ∇^2 is differential *Laplace operator*.

The differential equation for bending of thin elastic plates, known as *equation of Sophie Germain-Lagrange*, is obtained after investigating the equilibrium of a differential element of the plate. The plate is loaded with a perpendicular to its plane external load with intensity q, *figure 4.2*. In the figure are shown the forces, acting only in z coordinate direction.

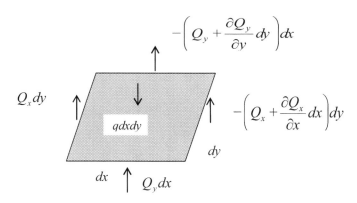

Figure 4.2: Vertical forces for a differential element of the plate

Let us write the equilibrium condition $\sum V = 0$ through the forces, acting perpendicularly to the plane of the element, using the assumption that the displacements are small. In that case we will get:

$$\frac{\partial Q_x}{\partial x} dxdy + \frac{\partial Q_y}{\partial y} dxdy = -qdxdy . \qquad (4.19)$$

Substituting eqs. (4.16) and (4.17) in (4.19) and dividing to the surface of the element $dxdy$ we get:

$$-D\frac{\partial^2}{\partial x^2}\nabla^2 w - D\frac{\partial^2}{\partial y^2}\nabla^2 w = -q(x, y), \qquad (4.20)$$

$$D\left(\frac{\partial^2}{\partial x^2}\nabla^2 w + \frac{\partial^2}{\partial y^2}\nabla^2 w\right) = D\left(\frac{\partial^2}{\partial x^2} + \frac{\partial^2}{\partial y^2}\right)\nabla^2 w = q(x, y) \qquad (4.21)$$

and

$$D\nabla^2\nabla^2 w = D\nabla^4 w = q\left(x, y\right). \tag{4.22}$$

$$D\left(\frac{\partial^4 w}{\partial x^4} + 2\frac{\partial^4 w}{\partial x^2\partial y^2} + \frac{\partial^4 w}{\partial y^4}\right) = q\left(x, y\right) \tag{4.23}$$

The expression (4.23) is fourth order partial differential equation with constant coefficients. It is known, as we have mentioned before, as *equation of Sophie Germain-Lagrange.* It gives in a direct form the relation between the vertical (transverse) displacement and the intensity of the load at a point of the plate. In terms to obtain the function, describing the displacements, this equation supposed to be integrated.

The problem has unique solution when the function we are searching for to represent the vertical displacement at the points of the middle plane of the plate $w\left(x, y\right)$, satisfies not only eq. (4.23) but specific boundary conditions, as well. These boundary conditions supposed to be four, because the differential equation is from the fourth order, and by type they could be kinematic—displacements and rotations, or static—forces or moments.

4.3 Theory of Reissner-Mindlin

The theory of Reissner-Mindlin, or known also as *theory for bending of moderate thick elastic plates,* is based on similar to the theory of Kirchoff assumptions, but with one principal difference in regards to the second of them. In the reviewed theory, this precondition states that:

- *Every segment with length h, perpendicular to the middle plane of the plate before the loading keeps its length, but it does not necessary remains perpendicular to the tangent towards the middle surface after the loading. The angle of its additional rotation is the shear strain of the section, in case that the shear stresses are constant in its elevation*

In this case for the displacements are valid the expressions:

$$u\left(x,y,z\right)=-z\sin\varphi_y\approx-ztg\varphi_y=-z\left(\frac{\partial w}{\partial x}-\gamma_{xz}\right)=-z\varphi_y, \quad (4.24)$$

$$v\left(x,y,z\right)=-z\left(\frac{\partial w}{\partial y}-\gamma_{yz}\right)=-z\varphi_x, \quad (4.25)$$

$$w\left(x,y,z\right)=w\left(x,y,0\right)=w_0, \quad (4.26)$$

and for the strains:

$$\varepsilon_x=\frac{\partial}{\partial x}u\left(x,y,z\right)=-z\frac{\partial}{\partial x}\left(\frac{\partial w}{\partial x}-\gamma_{xz}\right)=-z\frac{\partial}{\partial x}\varphi_y, \quad (4.27)$$

$$\varepsilon_y=\frac{\partial}{\partial y}v\left(x,y,z\right)=-z\frac{\partial}{\partial y}\left(\frac{\partial w}{\partial y}-\gamma_{yz}\right)=-z\frac{\partial}{\partial y}\varphi_x, \quad (4.28)$$

$$\gamma_{xy}=\frac{\partial}{\partial y}u\left(x,y,z\right)+\frac{\partial}{\partial x}v\left(x,y,z\right)=-z\left(\frac{\partial\varphi_y}{\partial y}+\frac{\partial\varphi_x}{\partial x}\right). \quad (4.29)$$

The index in functions φ_x and φ_y shows the direction of the vector of rotation.

The stresses at the points of the cross section are obtained from the Hooke's law:

$$\sigma_x = \frac{E}{1-\upsilon^2}\left(\varepsilon_x + \upsilon\varepsilon_y\right) = -\frac{Ez}{1-\upsilon^2}\left(\frac{\partial}{\partial x}\varphi_y + \upsilon\frac{\partial}{\partial y}\varphi_x\right), \qquad (4.30)$$

$$\sigma_y = \frac{E}{1-\upsilon^2}\left(\varepsilon_y + \upsilon\varepsilon_x\right) = -\frac{Ez}{1-\upsilon^2}\left(\frac{\partial}{\partial y}\varphi_x + \upsilon\frac{\partial}{\partial x}\varphi_y\right), \qquad (4.31)$$

$$\tau_{xy} = \tau_{yx} = G\gamma_{xy} = G\gamma_{yx} = -\frac{Ez}{1+\upsilon}\left(\frac{\partial\varphi_y}{\partial y} + \frac{\partial\varphi_x}{\partial x}\right). \qquad (4.32)$$

The relations, relevant to the theory of Reissner-Mindlin, could be transformed into the ones from the theory of Kirchoff, if $\gamma_{xz} = \gamma_{yz} = 0$ is used. In this way expressions as (4.24) and (4.25) for instance, are transformed into eq. (4.4) and eq. (4.5), i.e. absence of shear deformability due to shear forces. The deformability of shear forces supposes the result of larger in value vertical displacements, and at the same time lower in value normal stresses, and from there—bending moments.

4.4   Comparison of the vector of the displacements in bending of elastic plates theories.

We are going to give the vectors of the displacements at a point, related to the theory of Kirchoff, the theory of Reissner-Mindlin, and to third order theory. We are going to give the vectors, in case that there are also membrane stresses (membrane forces). That means an existence of strains in the middle plane of the plate.

1.   *Theory of Kirchhoff:*

$$\left\{\begin{matrix} u \\ v \\ w \end{matrix}\right\} = \left\{\begin{matrix} u(x,y,z) \\ v(x,y,z) \\ w(x,y,z) \end{matrix}\right\} = \left(\begin{matrix} u(x,y,0) - z\dfrac{\partial w}{\partial x} \\ v(x,y,0) - z\dfrac{\partial w}{\partial y} \\ w(x,y,0) \end{matrix}\right). \qquad (4.43)$$

2.   *Theory of Reissner-Mindlin:*

$$\left\{\begin{matrix} u \\ v \\ w \end{matrix}\right\} = \left\{\begin{matrix} u(x,y,z) \\ v(x,y,z) \\ w(x,y,z) \end{matrix}\right\} = \left(\begin{matrix} u(x,y,0) - z\varphi_y \\ v(x,y,0) - z\varphi_x \\ w(x,y,0) \end{matrix}\right). \qquad (4.44)$$

3.   *Theory of third order:*

$$\left\{\begin{matrix} u \\ v \\ w \end{matrix}\right\} = \left\{\begin{matrix} u(x,y,z) \\ v(x,y,z) \\ w(x,y,z) \end{matrix}\right\} = \left(\begin{matrix} u(x,y,0) - z\left[\varphi_y - \dfrac{4}{3}\left(\dfrac{z}{h}\right)^2\left(\dfrac{\partial w}{\partial x} - \varphi_y\right)\right] \\ v(x,y,0) - z\left[\varphi_x - \dfrac{4}{3}\left(\dfrac{z}{h}\right)^2\left(\dfrac{\partial w}{\partial y} - \varphi_x\right)\right] \\ w(x,y,0) \end{matrix}\right). \qquad (4.45)$$

In the theory of Kirchoff there is a numerical identity between the first derivative of the vertical displacement, and the rotation of the vertical cross section. In the theory of Reissner-Mindlin these quantities differ from the value of the shear strain. The displacements of the points of a vertical cross section, related to the theories of higher order, are not linear function of the coordinate z. For instance, in eq. (4.45) the distance of the point from the middle plane appears in its third power. It means that, the deformed shape of the cross section is more complex, and it is expressed by a cubic function. This distribution of displacements corresponds to the shear stresses, expressed by quadratic function. The idea is illustrated in *Figure 4.3*.

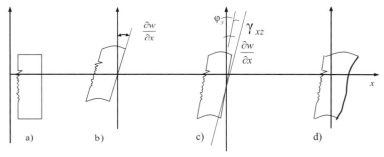

Figure 4.3: Deformation of the cross section, according to the various plate theories

a) – non-deformed cross section
b) – deformed cross section in the theory of Kirchhoff
c) – deformed cross section in the theory of Reissner-Mindlin
d) – deformed cross section in the theory of higher order.

$$\sigma_z(x,y) = \upsilon(\sigma_x(x,y) + \sigma_y(x,y)), \qquad (2.25)$$

$$\tau_{xy} = \tau_{yx} = \overline{G}\gamma_{xy} = \overline{G}\gamma_{yx}. \qquad (2.26)$$

The Method of double trigonometric series in bending of thin elastic plates (Navier method)

5.1 The idea of the Navier method

As we have already mentioned before, the possibilities for analytical solution of the differential equation for bending of thin plates

$$D\left(\frac{\partial^4 w}{\partial x^4} + 2\frac{\partial^4 w}{\partial x^2 \partial y^2} + \frac{\partial^4 w}{\partial y^4}\right) = q(x,y) \qquad (5.1)$$

are limited. They depend on the type, and the location of boundary conditions. There are known several analytical (called also classical) solutions, which are applicable to a narrow circle of problems. Each of these solutions, known also as methods, uses a different construction of the function of vertical (transverse) displacements. It is in accordance with specific boundary conditions. We are going to remind that under boundary conditions we assume not only kinematic, i.e. displacements and rotations, but also force (static) conditions, for instance, a presence or absence of bending moment, vertical force, etc. In these solutions mainly trigonometrical, or hyperbolo-trigonometrical functions are used. In some of the solutions exponential or polynomial series are introduced.

In this chapter we are going to introduce one of the most popular, and easy to be applied methods. This method is usable when a thin, smooth, rectangular plate is available, loaded with distributed load, and it is also supported in the lines of its contour. This method is known as *Navier method*. It is applicable in a case of linear elasticity of the material, because it uses a superposition of the effects of decomposed vertical (transverse) load.

Further down we well see that the load could be applied not only upon the entire plate, but upon a part of the plate, as well. This part though supposed to be in a rectangular shape. This has been predetermined by the integration of the load, used for the so-called decomposition. A similar quality was available in the method of trigonometric series, *Chapter 3*. The load in this method could be distributed only upon a part (segment) of disk's contour.

The function of the vertical displacement of the plate's middle plane is expressed through infinite trigonometrical series, more precisely: through double sum of infinite trigonometric series, type:

$$w(x,y,z) = w(x,y,0) = \sum_{p=1}^{\infty}\sum_{q=1}^{\infty} C_{pq} \sin\frac{p\pi}{a}x \sin\frac{q\pi}{b}y \qquad (5.2)$$

or

$$w(x,y,z) = w(x,y,0) = \sum_{p=1}^{\infty} C_{p} \sin\frac{p\pi}{a}x \sum_{q=1}^{\infty} C_{q} \sin\frac{q\pi}{b}y, \qquad (5.3)$$

where the coefficients C_{pq} or C_p and C_q are selected in a way to satisfy the Sophie Germain-Lagrange equation, (see *Chapter 4*). With a and b are expressed the measures of the plate. The coordinate system is placed in a way that, its sides are parallel to the coordinate directions x and y, respectively. This is illustrated in *Figure 5.1*. Expression, type (5.3), is allowed when the function of external load $q(x, y)$ could be expressed as $q(x, y) = q_x(x) q_y(y)$.

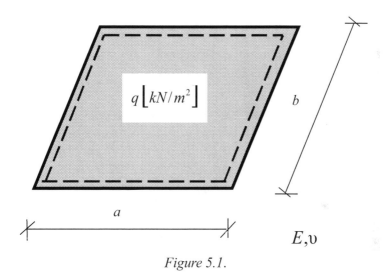

Figure 5.1.

We have mentioned already that the Navier method belongs to the so-called classical or analytical methods from Theory of elasticity. In expressions eq. (5.2) and eq. (5.3) the harmonic multipliers $\sin\dfrac{p\pi}{a}x$ and $\sin\dfrac{q\pi}{b}y$ are basis functions, and the coefficients C_{pq} or C_p and C_q could be considered as weight towards them. In the same way as in the method of trigonometrical series from the plane theory of elasticity, and here the weights are decay functions. Their values decrease with the increase of p and q. Since they are present not only in the vertical displacement function, but also in the expressions for the internal forces, we assume a quick convergence of the results. It is important to emphasize that, in so-called, classical methods the basis functions are defined into the entire domain, i.e. the entire geometry of the plate. On the contrary, the *Finite elements method*, which we will introduce in the next chapters, uses a discreet basis. It has been defined about specific subdomains, called finite elements.

The algorithm of the solution could be expressed as:

- *Choosing a function for expressing the vertical displacement of the points of plate's middle plan, relations (5.2) or (5.3);*
- *Obtaining the expressions of the rotations, bending moments, vertical forces, and the Sophie Germain-Lagrange equation, after using the selected function of vertical displacement. In these expressions take part first, second, third and forth (respectively) partial derivatives of the displacement, (see Chapter 4);*
- *Expressing the coefficients C_{pq} or C_p and C_q, where the decay of the load implicitly takes part, based on the Fourier integral transformation;*
- *Computing of: displacement, rotation, bending or torsional moments, vertical forces or intensity of the load, at a point through substituting of the coordinates of the point in the expressions of stages 1 or 2.*

The relations, concerning *stage 1,* have been already presented. Now we are going to present the expressions, correlating to *stage 2*, i.e. the ones related to: displacements, rotations, bending or torsional moments, vertical forces, and the *Sophie Germain-Lagrange equation.* These are the, shown below, dependencies from eq. (5.5) to eq. (5.12). They, as we can notice, always contain trigonometrical members (basis functions), in a form of sine or cosine functions, for instance, $\sin\dfrac{p\pi}{a}x$ and $\sin\dfrac{q\pi}{b}y$, changing only the weight multipliers. For instance: $C_{pq}\dfrac{p\pi}{a}$ and $C_{pq}\dfrac{q\pi}{b}$ respectively in $w^x(x,y,z)$ and $w^y(x,y,z)$; $\dfrac{D\pi^2}{a^2}C_{pq}\left(p^2+\upsilon\alpha^2q^2\right)$ and $\dfrac{D\pi^2}{a^2}C_{pq}\left(\upsilon p^2+\alpha^2q^2\right)$ respectively in $M_x(x,y)$ and $M_y(x,y)$,

etc. In these multipliers D is the cylindrical or plate stiffness, computed from expression (4.18), i.e. from:

$$D=\frac{Eh^3}{12\left(1-\upsilon^2\right)}, \tag{5.4}$$

and with α is expressed the relation a/b.

In *stage 3* the coefficients C_{pq} are selected in a way to satisfy the *Sophie Germain-Lagrange equation*. In *stage 4* we obtain specific values of the quantities we are interesting, after substituting the coordinates of the point for which the computation is performed.

Stage 3 could be individualized for each particular case of loading, and *stage 4* is connected with the location of the point.

As much as possible, the analytical formulation of the method could be applied towards a wider circle of problems, but the final expressions are highly dependent on, more specifically limited by, the type of boundary conditions. For other types of boundary conditions, for instance, fixed edges, it is supposed to be used a different type of the basis.

In a case of simply supported edges of the plate on its contour, periodicity of the basic trigonometric functions is used, i.e. of $\sin\dfrac{p\pi}{a}x$ and $\sin\dfrac{q\pi}{b}y$. The multipliers in front of current coordinates x and y ($\dfrac{p\pi}{a}$ and $\dfrac{q\pi}{b}$) ensure this periodicity to be in accordance with the geometrical measures of the plate. In this way we are going to have zero values for displacements, and bending moments in the contour lines, i.e. for lines $x = 0$ and $x = a$ or $y = 0$ and $y = b$, something we have already accentuated on.

So, if we select the function of the vertical displacement of the middle plane of the plate to be type eq. (5.2), then the expressions for: rotations, bending or torsional moments, shear forces, and the *Sophie Germain-Lagrange equation,* assuming that $\alpha = \dfrac{a}{b}$, obtain the form respectively:

- ***rotation in direction of coordinate axes:***

$$\frac{\partial}{\partial x} w(x, y, 0) = w^x(x, y) = \sum_{p=1}^{\infty} \sum_{q=1}^{\infty} C_{pq} \frac{p\pi}{a} \cos \frac{p\pi}{a} x \sin \frac{q\pi}{b} y , \quad (5.5)$$

$$\frac{\partial}{\partial y} w(x, y, 0) = w^y(x, y) = \sum_{p=1}^{\infty} \sum_{q=1}^{\infty} C_{pq} \frac{q\pi}{b} \sin \frac{p\pi}{a} x \cos \frac{q\pi}{b} y . \quad (5.6)$$

- ***bending and torsional moment:***

$$M_x(x, y, 0) = M_x(x, y) = \frac{D\pi^2}{a^2} \sum_{p=1}^{\infty} \sum_{q=1}^{\infty} C_{pq} \left(p^2 + \upsilon \alpha^2 q^2 \right) \sin \frac{p\pi}{a} x \sin \frac{q\pi}{b} y$$
$$(5.7)$$

$$M_y(x, y, 0) = M_y(x, y) = \frac{D\pi^2}{a^2} \sum_{p=1}^{\infty} \sum_{q=1}^{\infty} C_{pq} \left(\upsilon p^2 + \alpha^2 q^2 \right) \sin \frac{p\pi}{a} x \sin \frac{q\pi}{b} y$$
$$(5.8)$$

$$M_{xy}(x, y, 0) = M_{xy}(x, y) = -\frac{D\pi^2}{ab}(1 - \upsilon) \sum_{p=1}^{\infty} \sum_{q=1}^{\infty} C_{pq} pq \cos \frac{p\pi}{a} x \cos \frac{q\pi}{b} y$$
$$(5.9)$$

- ### *shear forces:*

$$Q_x(x,y,0) = Q_x(x,y) = \frac{D\pi^3}{a^3} \sum_{p=1}^{\infty} \sum_{q=1}^{\infty} C_{pq} \left(p^3 + \alpha^2 pq^2\right) \cos\frac{p\pi}{a}x \sin\frac{q\pi}{b}y$$

(5.10)

$$Q_y(x,y,0) = Q_y(x,y) = \frac{D\pi^3}{a^2 b} \sum_{p=1}^{\infty} \sum_{q=1}^{\infty} C_{pq} \left(p^2 q + \alpha^2 q^3\right) \sin\frac{p\pi}{a}x \cos\frac{q\pi}{b}y$$

(5.11)

- ### *The Sophie Germain-Lagrange equation:*

$$D\sum_{p=1}^{\infty} \sum_{q=1}^{\infty} C_{pq} \left(\frac{p^4 \pi^4}{a^4} + 2\frac{p^2 q^2 \pi^4}{a^2 b^2} + \frac{q^4 \pi^4}{b^4}\right) \sin\frac{p\pi}{a}x \sin\frac{q\pi}{b}y =$$
$$= q(x,y)$$

(5.12)

The expressions from eq. (5.8) to eq. (5.12) are given in a more general form, i.e. through coefficients C_{pq}.

Let us now convert the *Sophie Germain-Lagrange equation*, expressed through (5.12), assuming that $\alpha = \frac{a}{b}$. We obtain:

$$\sum_{p=1}^{\infty} \sum_{q=1}^{\infty} \frac{D\pi^4}{a^4} C_{pq} \left(p^2 + \alpha^2 q^2\right)^2 \sin\frac{p\pi}{a}x \sin\frac{q\pi}{b}y = q(x,y).$$ (5.13)

If now we place

$$q_{pq} = \frac{D\pi^4}{a^4} C_{pq} \left(p^2 + \alpha^2 q^2\right)^2, \text{ for } p = 1,2,3,... \text{ and } q = 1,2,3,... $$ (5.14)

in expression eq. (5.13), we obtain:

$$\sum_{p=1}^{\infty}\sum_{q=1}^{\infty} q_{pq} \sin\frac{p\pi}{a}x\sin\frac{q\pi}{b}y = q(x,y). \qquad (5.15.a)$$

In this expression q_{pq} denotes the coefficient of the decomposition of the load in a double trigonometric series. And here, if the load could be expressed as $q(x,y) = q_x(x)q_y(y)$, then relation eq. (5.15) we could convert into:

$$\sum_{p=1}^{\infty} q_p \sin\frac{p\pi}{a}x\sum_{q=1}^{\infty} q_q \sin\frac{q\pi}{b}y = q(x,y). \qquad (5.15.b)$$

We are familiar with the orthogonality of the sine functions. There is an exception only in the case when the amount of the semi-waves coincides. We are going to use it further down. Then we obtain:

$$q_{pq} = \frac{4}{ab}\int_0^a\int_0^b q(x,y)\sin\frac{p\pi}{a}x\sin\frac{q\pi}{b}ydxdy \text{ , for } p=1,2,3,... \text{ and}$$

$$q = 1,2,3,... \qquad (5.16.a)$$

or

$$q_{pq} = \frac{2}{a}\int_0^a q_x(x)\sin\frac{p\pi}{a}xdx\frac{2}{b}\int_0^b q_y(y)\sin\frac{q\pi}{b}ydy = I_x I_y \text{ , for}$$

$$p = 1,2,3,... \text{ and } q = 1,2,3,..., \qquad (5.16.b)$$

where: $I_x = \frac{2}{a}\int_0^a q_x(x)\sin\frac{p\pi}{a}xdx$ and $I_y = \frac{2}{b}\int_0^b q_y(y)\sin\frac{q\pi}{b}ydy$.

These integrals are identical with the integrals, used in the method of trigonometric series, (*see Chapter 3*). In practice, the possibility of the load to be expressed as a product of two functions, one with argument x, and the other with y, leads to significant computational relieves, and a certain analogy with the already known and cited method, used in the plane problem.

Based on eq. (5.14) we could express C_{pq}. Then we obtain that:

$$C_{pq} = q_{pq} \frac{a^4}{D\pi^4 \left(p^2 + \alpha^2 q^2\right)^2}, \text{ for } p = 1, 2, 3, \ldots \text{ and } q = 1, 2, 3, \ldots$$
$$(5.17)$$

Once being specified, these coefficients could be substituted in relations: from eq. (5.5) to eq. (5.12), for computing of the researched quantities at a specific point. For this purpose we introduce its coordinates.

So far we have shown how the results from *stage 3* could be substituted in the expressions of *stage 2* until achieving the final dependencies, used to obtain the searched numerical value of specific quantity at the corresponding point.

5.2   Other methods (Method of Maurice Levy)

At the beginning of this chapter we said that other type of boundary conditions could be satisfied if there is an appropriate for this purpose construction of the function, describing the displacements. That means a different support in the edge of the rectangular plate. We were already convinced that this role plays the so-called basis. We are going to research a possibility like that, where two of the opposite sides are simply supported and in the other two there could be: arbitrary supported or free contours. This method is known also as *method of Maurice Levy*, and finds a wider application than the Navier method.

We are going to demonstrate this method strictly fundamentally. The function of vertical displacements is selected as:

$$w(x, y, z) = w(x, y, 0) = \sum_{p=1}^{\infty} Y_p(y) \sin\frac{p\pi}{a}x. \qquad (5.18)$$

In this construction $\sin\dfrac{p\pi}{a}x$ is a basis in axis x, which ensures the satisfaction of the boundary conditions, i.e. both of the two simply supported sides. They are parallel to axis y. The basis consists of trigonometric multipliers $\sin\dfrac{p\pi}{a}x$. The function $Y_p(y)$ is searched in such a way, so it could be able to satisfy *the Sophie Germain-Lagrange equation*, and the boundary conditions, or:

$$Y_p^{IV}(y) - 2\alpha_p^2 Y_p^{II}(y) + \alpha_p^4 Y_p(y) = B_p(y). \qquad (5.19)$$

Chapter 6

Introduction to the linear theory of thin elastic shells

6.1 Classification and basic assumptions in the linear theory of thin elastic shells

We define three different kinds of shells:

*   *cylindrical;*
*   *spherical;*
*   *shells with double curvature.*

The model of cylindrical shell is used for computing of tanks, store-pits, pipes, etc. The spherical shells are common in many architectural visions as domes, etc. The shell with double curvature can be treated as a general case of shell configuration.

Besides the thin elastic shells, we know also: thick and very thick shells. Here the deformability of the cross section due to the shear forces must be taken into account.

One possible classification of shells is based on the relation between its thickness h towards the smallest supporting distance R (or supporting contour), i.e. h / R. Then the shells we classify as:

- *very thin shells* $\dfrac{h}{R} < \dfrac{1}{200}$,

- *thin shells* $\dfrac{1}{200} < \dfrac{h}{R} < \dfrac{1}{25}$,

- *thick shells* $\dfrac{1}{25} < \dfrac{h}{R} < \dfrac{1}{10}$,

- *very thick shells* $\dfrac{1}{10} < \dfrac{h}{R} < \dfrac{1}{5}$.

6.2   A mathematical model of thin elastic shell

The shell is a three-dimensional solid, which behavior, based on specific assumptions, we are going to express through surface. This surface is *the middle surface* of the shell. It is formed by the all points—equally spaced from the upper and the lower surface.

We are going to briefly review the mathematical model of the thin elastic shell. It follows the principal idea, used in the theory of thin plates, *(see Chapter 4)*. The second of these assumptions is expressed here as:

- *Every segment with length h, perpendicular to the middle surface of the shell before the loading, keeps its length and remains perpendicular to the tangent towards the middle surface, formed after the loading.*

Based on all three of the assumptions, the displacements, and from there, the strains and the stresses at every point of the shell could be defined through the displacements of the points of the middle surface.

Let us review a differential element of the shell around a point. The forces, acting upon it for a unit of length, in the presence of load, and shown upon the differential element, are illustrated in *Figure 6.1*.

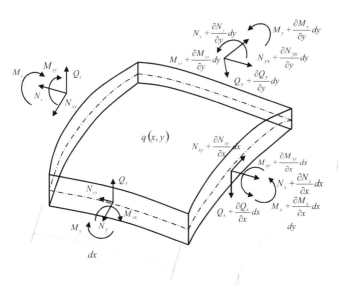

Figure 6.1. Equilibrium of differential element of the shell.

6.2.1 Expressing the strains (strains-displacements relations)

The strains at a point could be expressed through the strains of the middle surface ε^0, coordinate z of the point from the same surface, and two radii. Then, for the strains ε_x and ε_y we get, respectively:

$$\varepsilon_x = \varepsilon_x^0 - z\left(\frac{1}{r_x^R} - \frac{1}{r_x^I}\right) = \varepsilon_x^0 - z\chi_x^{R-I} \tag{6.1}$$

and

$$\varepsilon_y = \varepsilon_y^0 - z\left(\frac{1}{r_y^R} - \frac{1}{r_y^I}\right) = \varepsilon_y^0 - z\chi_y^{R-I}, \tag{6.2}$$

where: ε_x^0 and ε_y^0 are the strains, respectively, in axis x and y of the middle surface of the shell; r_x^I and r_x^R are the radii of curvature in axis x, valid for the non-deformed and the deformed middle surface; analogical are the symbols for the radii r_y^I and r_y^R, but in axis y. With χ_x^{R-I} and χ_y^{R-I} are expressed the changes of the curvature.

The shear strain derives from:

$$\gamma_{xy} = \gamma_{xy}^0 - 2z\chi_{xy}^{R-I}, \tag{6.3}$$

where γ_{xy}^0 is the shear strain at a point, and χ_{xy}^{R-I} we will call *torsion curvature* of the middle surface.

6.2.2 Expressing the stresses (stresses-strains relations)

The stresses derive from:

$$\sigma_x = \frac{E}{1-\upsilon^2}\left[\varepsilon_x^0 + \upsilon\varepsilon_y^0 - z\left(\chi_x^{R-I} + \upsilon\chi_y^{R-I}\right)\right], \tag{6.4}$$

$$\sigma_y = \frac{E}{1-\upsilon^2}\left[\varepsilon_y^0 + \upsilon\varepsilon_x^0 - z\left(\chi_y^{R-I} + \upsilon\chi_x^{R-I}\right)\right] \quad \text{and} \tag{6.5}$$

$$\tau_{xy} = G\left(\tau_{xy}^0 - 2z\chi_{xy}^{R-I}\right). \tag{6.6}$$

In the above formulas E and υ are the already known, respectively: modulus of elasticity and Poisson's ratio, and

$$G = \frac{E}{2(1+\upsilon)}.$$

If the initial curvatures are zeros, or the initial radii of curvatures are infinity, then relations eqs. (6.4), (6.5) and (6.6) are identical with eqs. (4.10), (4.11) and (4.12), respectively, *(see Chapter 4)*.

6.2.3 Generalized forces

The generalized forces can be expressed as:

$$N_x = \frac{Eh}{1-\upsilon^2}\left(\varepsilon_x^0 + \upsilon\varepsilon_y^0\right), \tag{6.9}$$

$$N_y = \frac{Eh}{1-\upsilon^2}\left(\varepsilon_y^0 + \upsilon\varepsilon_x^0\right), \tag{6.10}$$

$$N_{xy} = N_{yx} = \frac{Eh}{2(1+\upsilon)}\gamma_{xy}^0, \tag{6.11}$$

$$M_x = -D\left(\chi_x^{R-I} + \upsilon\chi_y^{R-I}\right) = -\frac{Eh^3}{12(1-\upsilon^2)}\left(\chi_x^{R-I} + \upsilon\chi_y^{R-I}\right) \tag{6.12}$$

$$M_y = -D\left(\chi_y^{R-I} + \upsilon\chi_x^{R-I}\right) = -\frac{Eh^3}{12(1-\upsilon^2)}\left(\chi_y^{R-I} + \upsilon\chi_x^{R-I}\right) \tag{6.13}$$

$$M_{xy} = M_{yx} = -D\left(1-\upsilon\right)\chi_{xy}^{R-I}. \tag{6.14}$$

Here eqs. (6.12), (6.13) and (6.14) we could review as a generalization, respectively of eqs. (4.13), (4.14) and (4.15).

6.3 Elements of the theory of thin shallow shells

For shallow shells we assume these shells for which $\frac{f_{max}}{R} \leq \frac{1}{5}$, where f_{max} is the maximum altitude.

If the loading is a vertical load, then the equilibrium equations we could express as:

$$\frac{\partial N_x}{\partial x} + \frac{\partial N_{xy}}{\partial y} = 0, \qquad (6.22)$$

$$\frac{\partial N_y}{\partial y} + \frac{\partial N_{yx}}{\partial x} = 0, \qquad (6.23)$$

$$\frac{\partial M_x}{\partial x} + \frac{\partial M_{xy}}{\partial y} - Q_x = 0, \qquad (6.24)$$

$$\frac{\partial M_y}{\partial y} + \frac{\partial M_{yx}}{\partial x} - Q_y = 0 \qquad \text{and} \qquad (6.25)$$

$$\frac{\partial^2 M_x}{\partial x^2} + 2\frac{\partial^2 M_{xy}}{\partial x \partial y} + \frac{\partial^2 M_y}{\partial y^2} + \frac{N_x}{r_x} + \frac{N_y}{r_y} + 2\frac{N_{xy}}{r_{xy}} = q(x,y). \quad (6.26)$$

where N_x, N_y, N_{xy}, N_{yx}, Q_x and Q_y are generalized forces, and with r and specified index are expressed the radii, *Figure 6.2*.

It is obvious that, if the radii towards infinity, eq. (6.26) can be transformed into eq. (4.23).

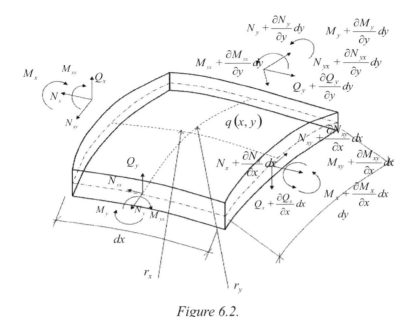

Figure 6.2.

Here could be entered functions of *Airy*, and through them to express N_x, N_y and $N_{xy} = N_{yx}$. For instance:

$$N_x = \frac{\partial^2 \varphi(x, y)}{\partial y^2}, \tag{6.27}$$

$$N_y = \frac{\partial^2 \varphi(x, y)}{\partial x^2}, \tag{6.28}$$

$$N_{xy} = \frac{\partial^2 \varphi(x, y)}{\partial x \partial y} - C(x) \qquad \text{and} \tag{6.29}$$

$$N_{yx} = \frac{\partial^2 \varphi(x, y)}{\partial x \partial y} - C(y), \tag{6.30}$$

where $C(x)$ and $C(y)$ are correction functions.

The equation for continuity of strains can be expresses as:

$$\frac{\partial^2 \varepsilon_x}{\partial y^2} + \frac{\partial^2 \varepsilon_y}{\partial x^2} - \frac{\partial^2 \gamma_{xy}}{\partial x \partial y} + \frac{1}{r_x}\frac{\partial^2 w}{\partial y^2} - 2\frac{1}{r_{xy}}\frac{\partial^2 w}{\partial x \partial y} + \frac{1}{r_y}\frac{\partial^2 w}{\partial x^2} = 0 . \quad (6.32)$$

The equation for equilibrium of differential element is:

$$\nabla_r^2 F + D^s \nabla^2 \nabla^2 w = q(x, y), \quad (6.33)$$

where $D^s \equiv D$ is the cylindrical stiffness of the shell.

6.3 Theory of spherical shells

We are going to use polar coordinates ρ and θ. With them we express the projections upon horizontal plane. Then ρ is the projection of the polar radius, and θ is the horizontal angle of this projection towards the coordinate axis x, *(see Figure 6.3.)*.

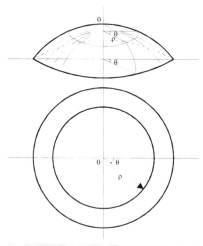

Figure 6.3. Spherical shell

If we choose an auxiliary function, denoted as Φ, through which we could express the vertical displacements $w(\rho,\theta)$ as:

$$w(\rho,\theta) = \nabla^2\nabla^2\Phi(\rho,\theta) \qquad (6.37)$$

and function N (auxiliary), through which are given the stresses or the generalized forces, and its connection with Φ is:

$$N(\rho,\theta) = \frac{Eh}{R^2}\nabla^2\Phi(\rho,\theta) \qquad (6.38)$$

the equilibrium of the differential element we could express as:

$$D\nabla^2\nabla^2\nabla^2\nabla^2\Phi(\rho,\theta) + \frac{Eh}{R^2}\nabla^2\nabla^2\Phi(\rho,\theta) - p(\rho,\theta) = 0 \quad (6.39)$$

or

$$D\nabla^2\nabla^2 w(\rho,\theta) + \frac{Eh}{R^2}w(\rho,\theta) - p(\rho,\theta) = 0. \qquad (6.40)$$

In the above expressions h is thickness of the shell, R—the radius of the sphere, and $p(\rho,\theta)$ is the intensity of the load, radial in character.

The generalized forces, given to the middle surface of the spherical shell, which we denote as N_ρ, N_θ and S derive from the expressions:

$$N_\rho = \frac{1}{\rho}\frac{\partial N}{\partial\rho} + \frac{1}{\rho^2}\frac{\partial^2 N}{\partial\theta^2},$$

$$N_\theta = \frac{\partial^2 N}{\partial \rho^2} \qquad \text{and}$$

$$S = N_{xy} = N_{yx} - \frac{1}{\rho} \frac{\partial^2 N}{\partial \theta \partial \rho} + \frac{1}{\rho^2} \frac{\partial N}{\partial \theta}. \qquad (6.41)$$

The forces N_ρ, N_θ and $S = N_{xy} = N_{yx}$ are illustrated in *Figure 6.4.*

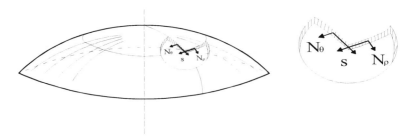

Figure 6.4.

6.5   Theory of thin cylindrical shells

This theory is widely covered in the literature. Here we are going to directly give the expressions through which they could be calculated, see expressions (6.42).

The geometry of the cylindrical shell is shown in *Figure 6.5.*

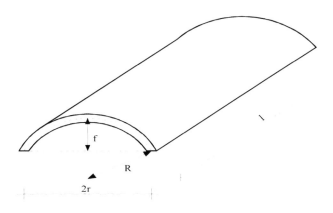

Figure 6.5.

$$N_x = \frac{Eh}{1-\upsilon^2}\left\{\frac{\partial u}{\partial x}+\upsilon\frac{\partial v}{\partial y}-\upsilon\frac{w}{R}+h^2\frac{1}{3R}\left[\frac{1-\upsilon-\upsilon^2}{1-\upsilon}\frac{\partial^2 w}{\partial x^2}-\frac{\upsilon}{1-\upsilon}\left(\frac{\partial^2 w}{\partial y^2}+\frac{w}{R^2}\right)\right]\right\},$$

$$N_y = \frac{Eh}{1-\upsilon^2}\left\{\upsilon\frac{\partial u}{\partial x}+\frac{\partial v}{\partial y}-\upsilon\frac{w}{R}+h^2\frac{1}{3R}\left[\frac{\upsilon^2}{1-\upsilon}\frac{\partial^2 w}{\partial x^2}+\frac{1}{1-\upsilon}\left(\frac{\partial^2 w}{\partial y^2}+\frac{w}{R^2}\right)\right]\right\},$$

$$N_{xy} = \frac{1-\upsilon}{2}\frac{Eh}{1-\upsilon^2}\left\{\frac{\partial v}{\partial x}+\frac{\partial u}{\partial y}+h^2\frac{1}{3R}\left[\frac{\partial^2 w}{\partial x\partial y}+\frac{1}{R}\frac{\partial v}{\partial x}\right]\right\},$$

$$N_{yx} = \frac{1-\upsilon}{2}\frac{Eh}{1-\upsilon^2}\left\{\frac{\partial v}{\partial x}+\frac{\partial u}{\partial y}-h^2\frac{1}{3R}\left[\frac{\partial^2 w}{\partial x\partial y}-\frac{1}{R}\frac{\partial u}{\partial y}\right]\right\},$$

and

$$M_x = -D\left(\frac{\partial^2 w}{\partial x^2}+\upsilon\frac{\partial^2 w}{\partial y^2}+\frac{1}{R}\frac{\partial u}{\partial x}+\frac{\upsilon}{R}\frac{\partial v}{\partial y}\right),$$

$$M_y = -D\left(\upsilon \frac{\partial^2 w}{\partial x^2} + \frac{\partial^2 w}{\partial y^2} + \frac{w}{R^2} \right),$$

$$M_{xy} = -\frac{1-\upsilon}{2}D\left(2\frac{\partial^2 w}{\partial x \partial y} + \frac{2}{R}\frac{\partial v}{\partial x} \right),$$

$$M_{yx} = -\frac{1-\upsilon}{2}D\left(2\frac{\partial^2 w}{\partial x \partial y} + \frac{1}{R}\frac{\partial v}{\partial x} - \frac{1}{R}\frac{\partial u}{\partial y} \right), \qquad (6.42)$$

where $D = \dfrac{Eh^3}{12\left(1-\upsilon^2\right)}$.

And here if $R \to \infty$, then eqs. (6.42) are identical with those, known from the theory of bending of thin elastic plates with membrane forces, and to those from the Kirchhoff's theory, related to the bending moments. The latest was discussed in *Chapter 4*.

Chapter **7**

Introduction to the
Finite element method (FEM)

7.1   The idea and the computing realization of the FEM

In *Chapter 2* and *Chapter 4* we discussed that a solution of basic problems in the *Theory of Elasticity* we could obtain through: a suitable choice of basis (basis functions-satisfying the boundary conditions) and weight coefficients. The basis was defined for the entire domain.

Another way for obtaining a solution is through dividing the domain into smaller domains, called *subdomains*. Suitable approximation of the solution we obtain when the entire domain has been presented as an assemblage of subdomains. In the subdomain the solution is based on smaller basis. The Finite element method (FEM) is similar computational technology. The subdomains are called *finite elements*, and the division of the domain—*discretisation of the domain*. In such techniques legitimately raise the question of the continuity of the unknown functions and their derivatives between the elements.

The FEM computational algorithm is:

1. Defining the geometry of the model. From mathematical point of view, this is the domain of the solution.
2. Assigning material characteristics.

Dividing the geometry of the model. Normally simplified geometrical forms (subdomains) are used, called *finite elements*. For two-dimensional zones: triangles, rectangles or quadrilateral, and in three-dimensional case: pyramids, parallelepipeds or prisms.

3. Selecting the model of the finite element. This represents a selection of basis functions, type: $\varphi_j(x, y, z)$, defined in the finite element domain, and the corresponding weight coefficients u_j. In the FEM this means selection of independent nodal parameters and corresponding approximation polynomials.

4. Formulating the supports and loading, from mathematical point of view—boundary conditions.

5. Solving the system of equations, and obtaining the values of the unknown (up to that point) weight coefficients u_j, expressed primarily through the vector of displacements.

6. Computing of the strains and stresses.

7. Interpretation of the results.

7.2 Basic relations of the FEM, illustrated upon beam element

The coefficients of stiffness of a beam element, arranged in a specific way, form matrix, called: *stiffness matrix* of the beam finite element.

In *Figure 7.1* are shown two beam elements, respectively with two or three nodes, located in the direction of coordinate axis *x*.

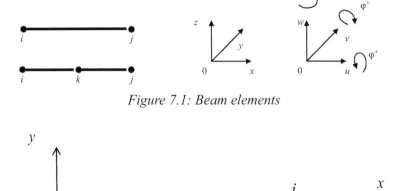

Figure 7.1: Beam elements

Figure 7.2: Beam element with two nodes

Suppose the finite element in *Figure 7.2* with bending and axial stiffness, denoted respectively as *EI* and *EA*, and possible displacements only in direction of coordinate axes *x* and *y*. The stiffness coefficients can be calculated using four deformed shapes of the element, corresponding to unit transverse displacement and unit rotation at node *i* and *j*, respectively. The deformed shapes, related to node *i* are illustrated in *Figure 7.3 and Figure 7.4*.

Figure 7.3.

Figure 7.4

The deformed shapes are expressed by cubic polynomials, called Hermit polynomials:

$$\phi_2(x) = 1 - 3\left(\frac{x}{l}\right)^2 + 2\left(\frac{x}{l}\right)^3 \tag{7.1}$$

and

$$\phi_3(x) = x\left(1 - \frac{x}{l}\right)^2. \tag{7.2}$$

for unit transverse displacement and unit rotation at node *i* and

$$\phi_5(x) = 3\left(\frac{x}{l}\right)^2 - 2\left(\frac{x}{l}\right)^3 \tag{7.3}$$

and

$$\phi_6(x) = \frac{x^2}{l}\left(\frac{x}{l} - 1\right). \tag{7.4}$$

for unit transverse displacement and unit rotation at node *j*.

Through these four functions, the transverse displacement at any point of the element with coordinate *x,* can be obtained from:

$$v(x) = \phi_2(x)v_1 + \phi_3(x)\phi_1 + \phi_5(x)v_j + \phi_6(x)\phi_j. \quad (7.5)$$

The coefficients v and ϕ are the displacements and rotations of the nodes, and they are analogical to the weight coefficients u_j from the previous item. The eq. (7.5) is linear combination of functions $\phi_2(x)$, $\phi_3(x)$, $\phi_5(x)$ and $\phi_6(x)$, treated as a basis. In the FEM the above functions are called: *shape functions*. In a similar way we can obtain the shape functions, corresponding to unit horizontal displacement, respectively at the left or the right node of the element. They are expressed as:

$$\phi_1(x) = 1 - \frac{x}{l} \quad (7.6)$$

and

$$\phi_4(x) = \frac{x}{l}. \quad (7.7)$$

The stiffness coefficients are equal to the reactions in virtual connections in the directions of the possible nodal displacements and rotations, called *degrees of freedom* of the element. The coefficients could be obtained by application of *the principle of virtual work*. We are going to show only the final expression for the bending terms:

$$\kappa_{ij} = \int_0^l EI\phi_i''(x)\phi_j''(x)dx. \quad (7.8)$$

The stiffness matrix of beam element derives from the expression:

$$[K_e] = \begin{bmatrix} \dfrac{EA}{l} & 0 & 0 & -\dfrac{EA}{l} & 0 & 0 \\[2mm] 0 & \dfrac{12EI}{l^3} & -\dfrac{6EI}{l^2} & 0 & -\dfrac{12EI}{l^3} & -\dfrac{6EI}{l^2} \\[2mm] 0 & -\dfrac{6EI}{l^2} & \dfrac{4EI}{l} & 0 & \dfrac{6EI}{l^2} & \dfrac{2EI}{l} \\[2mm] -\dfrac{EA}{l} & 0 & 0 & \dfrac{EA}{l} & 0 & 0 \\[2mm] 0 & -\dfrac{12EI}{l^3} & \dfrac{6EI}{l^2} & 0 & \dfrac{12EI}{l^3} & \dfrac{6EI}{l^2} \\[2mm] 0 & -\dfrac{6EI}{l^2} & \dfrac{2EI}{l} & 0 & \dfrac{6EI}{l^2} & \dfrac{4EI}{l} \end{bmatrix}. \quad (7.9)$$

The equilibrium equations of the beam element is:

$$\begin{bmatrix} \dfrac{EA}{l} & 0 & 0 & -\dfrac{EA}{l} & 0 & 0 \\[2mm] 0 & \dfrac{12EI}{l^3} & -\dfrac{6EI}{l^2} & 0 & -\dfrac{12EI}{l^3} & -\dfrac{6EI}{l^2} \\[2mm] 0 & -\dfrac{6EI}{l^2} & \dfrac{4EI}{l} & 0 & \dfrac{6EI}{l^2} & \dfrac{2EI}{l} \\[2mm] -\dfrac{EA}{l} & 0 & 0 & \dfrac{EA}{l} & 0 & 0 \\[2mm] 0 & -\dfrac{12EI}{l^3} & \dfrac{6EI}{l^2} & 0 & \dfrac{12EI}{l^3} & \dfrac{6EI}{l^2} \\[2mm] 0 & -\dfrac{6EI}{l^2} & \dfrac{2EI}{l} & 0 & \dfrac{6EI}{l^2} & \dfrac{4EI}{l} \end{bmatrix} \begin{Bmatrix} u_i \\ v_i \\ \phi_i \\ u_j \\ v_j \\ \phi_j \end{Bmatrix} = \begin{Bmatrix} F_i^x \\ F_i^y \\ M_i \\ F_j^x \\ F_j^y \\ M_j \end{Bmatrix}. \quad (7.10)$$

7.3   Basic relations of the FEM for three-dimensional body

The basic relations of the FEM for 3D case can be obtained, using the *Principle of virtual work* of the 3D body. Then:

$$\int_V \sigma^T \delta \varepsilon \, dV = \int_V \mathbf{f}^T \delta \mathbf{u} \, dV + \int_S \mathbf{p}^T \delta \mathbf{u} \, dS, \tag{7.11}$$

where σ, ε and **u** are respectively vectors of stresses, strains and displacements at a point of the body, **f** and **p** are vectors of components of the volume forces and distributed surface loads, and V and S are respectively the volume and the surface of the body. For Cartesian coordinate system, vectors σ and ε are expressed as:

$$\sigma = \{\sigma\} = \begin{Bmatrix} \sigma_x \\ \sigma_y \\ \sigma_z \\ \tau_{xy} \\ \tau_{xz} \\ \tau_{yz} \end{Bmatrix} \tag{7.12}$$

and

$$\varepsilon = \{\varepsilon\} = \begin{Bmatrix} \varepsilon_x \\ \varepsilon_y \\ \varepsilon_z \\ \gamma_{xy} \\ \gamma_{xz} \\ \gamma_{yz} \end{Bmatrix}. \tag{7.13}$$

77

The symbol δ in expression (7.11) indicates an infinitesimal kinematic change of the corresponding quantity.

From *The Theory of Elasticity* the variations of the stresses and strains at a point of the body can be expressed as:

$$\delta\sigma = \mathbf{D}\partial_0\delta\mathbf{u} \qquad\qquad (7.14)$$

and

$$\delta\varepsilon = \partial_0\delta\mathbf{u} , \qquad\qquad (7.15)$$

where ∂_0 is *matrix-differential operator of Laplace*.

If we divide the three-dimensional domain of the body, see *Figure 7.5.*, into finite number of subdomains, connected at individual points, called *nodes*, we perform *discretisation of the domain, (see Figure 7.6.).*

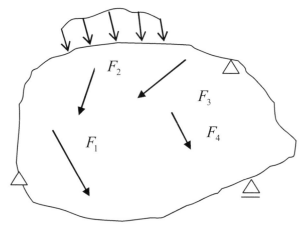

Figure 7.5. Three-dimensional body

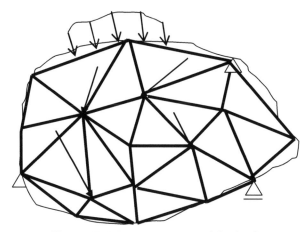

Figure 7.6. Discretisation of the body

Let us assume that, there are functions, from mathematical point of view *operators*, and through them we could obtain the displacement at any given point of the interior of the element, knowing the vector of nodal displacements. In this case we can write that:

$$\mathbf{u}_e\left(x, y, z\right) = \mathbf{N}_e\left(x, y, z\right)\mathbf{u}_e, \tag{7.16}$$

where, for clarity, $\mathbf{u}_{ie}$ has been substituted with $\mathbf{u}_e$, and the individual terms of $\mathbf{N}_e\left(x, y, z\right)$ are, the already mentioned, *shape functions*. They form *the matrix of shape functions* $\mathbf{N}_e$ of the element.

The virtual work of the three-dimensional body, upon discretisation through *n*-finite elements, derives from (7.13), considering (7.14), (7.15) and (7.16), can be expressed as:

$$\sum_{e=1}^{n}\left[\int_{V_e}\sigma_e^{\mathrm{T}}(x,y,z)\mathbf{B}_e(x,y,z)\delta\mathbf{u}_e dV_e\right]=$$

$$=\sum_{e=1}^{n}\left[\int_{V_e}\mathbf{f}_e^{\mathrm{T}}(x,y,z)\mathbf{N}_e(x,y,z)\delta\mathbf{u}_e dV_e+\int_{S_e}\mathbf{p}_e^{\mathrm{T}}(x,y,z)\mathbf{N}_e(x,y,z)\delta\mathbf{u}_e dS_e\right]$$

(7.17)

where for the matrix $\mathbf{B}_e(x,y,z)$ is valid the relation:

$$\mathbf{B}_e(x,y,z)=\partial_0\mathbf{N}_e(x,y,z).$$ (7.18)

The vector of stresses in the element we could express as:

$$\sigma_e(x,y,z)=\mathbf{D}\varepsilon_e(x,y,z)=\mathbf{D}\partial_0\mathbf{u}_e(x,y,z)=\mathbf{D}\mathbf{B}_e(x,y,z)\mathbf{u}_e.$$

(7.19)

Using (7.19) we could express (7.17) as:

$$\sum_{e=1}^{n}\left\{\mathbf{u}_e^{T}\left[\int_{V_e}\mathbf{B}_e^{\mathrm{T}}(x,y,z)\mathbf{D}\mathbf{B}_e(x,y,z)dV_e\right]\delta\mathbf{u}_e\right\}=$$

$$=\sum_{e=1}^{n}\left\{\left[\int_{V_e}\mathbf{f}_e^{\mathrm{T}}(x,y,z)\mathbf{N}_e(x,y,z)dV_e+\int_{S_e}\mathbf{p}_e^{\mathrm{T}}(x,y,z)\mathbf{N}_e(x,y,z)dS_e\right]\delta\mathbf{u}_e\right\}$$

(7.20)

If we introduce the following:

$$\mathbf{K}_e=\int_{V_e}\mathbf{B}_e^{\mathrm{T}}(x,y,z)\mathbf{D}\mathbf{B}_e(x,y,z)dV_e,$$ (7.21)

$$\mathbf{F}_e=\int_{V_e}\mathbf{f}_e^{\mathrm{T}}(x,y,z)\mathbf{N}_e(x,y,z)dV_e,$$ (7.22)

$$\mathbf{P}_e = \int_{S_e} \mathbf{p}_e^{T}(x, y, z) \mathbf{N}_e(x, y, z) dS_e ,\tag{7.23}$$

and eliminate the variational term, we get:

$$\mathbf{K}_e \mathbf{u}_e = \mathbf{F}_e + \mathbf{P}_e ,\tag{7.24}$$

where: $\mathbf{K}_e$ is stiffness matrix of the finite element,

$\mathbf{u}_e$ is vector of nodal displacements of the element,

$\mathbf{F}_e$ is vector of nodal forces, due to volume external loads,

$\mathbf{P}_e$ is vector of nodal forces, due to surface external loads.

The individual terms of $\mathbf{K}_e$ derive from the expression:

$$\kappa_{ij} = \int_{V_e} B_i^{T}(x, y, z) DB_j(x, y, z) dV_e ,\tag{7.25}$$

where i and j are degrees of freedom of the element.

Then for the entire body we can write that:

$$\mathbf{Ku} = \mathbf{F} + \mathbf{P} .\tag{7.26}$$

Relation (7.26) is the basic relation in the FEM.

If inertial forces are taken into account:

$$\int_{V} \sigma^{T} \delta \varepsilon dV = \int_{V} \mathbf{f}^{T} \delta \mathbf{u} dV + \int_{S} \mathbf{p}^{T} \delta \mathbf{u} dS - \int_{V} \rho \left(\frac{\partial^2}{\partial t^2} \mathbf{u} \right)^{T} \delta \mathbf{u} dV .\tag{7.27}$$

Here the corresponding vectors of the displacements, strains and stresses depend on the time. In this way eq. (7.20) yields to:

$$\sum_{e=1}^{n}\left\{\mathbf{u_e}^\mathrm{T}(t)\left[\int_{V_e}\mathbf{B_e}^\mathrm{T}(x,y,z)\mathbf{DB_e}(x,y,z)dV_e\right]\delta\mathbf{u_e}(t)\right\}=$$

$$=\sum_{e=1}^{n}\left\{\left[\int_{V_e}\mathbf{f_e}^\mathrm{T}(x,y,z,t)\mathbf{N_e}(x,y,z)dV_e+\int_{S_e}\mathbf{p_e}^\mathrm{T}(x,y,z,t)\mathbf{N_e}(x,y,z)dS_e\right]\delta\mathbf{u_e}(t)\right\}-$$

$$-\sum_{e=1}^{n}\ddot{\mathbf{u}}_e^\mathrm{T}(t)\left[\int_{V_e}\rho(x,y,z)\mathbf{N_e}^\mathrm{T}(x,y,z)\mathbf{N_e}(x,y,z)dV_e\right]\delta\mathbf{u_e}(t)$$

$$(7.28)$$

Then, if we introduce the following:

$$\mathbf{M_e}=\int_{V_e}\rho(x,y,z)\mathbf{N_e}^\mathrm{T}(x,y,z)\mathbf{N_e}(x,y,z)dV_e,\qquad(7.29)$$

the basis relations for the individual finite element are:

$$\mathbf{M_e}\ddot{\mathbf{u}}_e+\mathbf{K_e}\mathbf{u_e}=\mathbf{F_e}+\mathbf{P_e},\qquad(7.30)$$

and for the entire domain:

$$\mathbf{M\ddot{u}}+\mathbf{Ku}=\mathbf{F}+\mathbf{P}.\qquad(7.31)$$

8.5   Types of finite elements

In the application of the FEM for structural analysis numerous finite elements are used from the groups: *one-dimensional, two-dimensional and three-dimensional*, and some *special* types of finite elements, as well. The corresponding stiffness matrixes could be obtained in several ways as: direct approach, the principle of virtual work, through additional energy in element's domain, etc.

In the formulation of each type of finite elements several consecutive steps are distinguished. These steps are:

- *Defining the domain (geometry) of the finite element.*
- *Choosing and expressing the independent variables in the already defined domain.* These are the unknown quantities of the Method. In the structural finite elements, as we have already mentioned, these are mostly displacements and rotations.
- *Expressing the strains through the independent variables,* nodal displacements and rotations.
- *Expressing the stresses through the independent variables,* nodal displacements and rotations.
- *Forming the stiffness matrix.* That could be achieved by using some of the above-mentioned principles.
- *Obtaining the vector of nodal forces.* By nature this represents a procedure of obtaining the equivalent to the external loading forces. They could be found in directions, corresponding to the degrees of freedom of the element.
- *Forming the basis equations of the finite element.* In the structural finite elements these are the expressions of equilibrium in direction of the degrees of freedom. Arranged in groups, they form a system of linear equations of equilibrium, related to the degrees of freedom of the entire domain of the problem, the entire body or system of bodies.

Chapter 8

Stability of elastic structures

8.1   Introduction

In Structural mechanics we consider three types of equilibrium: *stable, neutrally stable* and *unstable, Figure 8.1.*

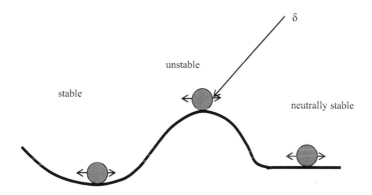

Figure 8.1. Types of equilibrium.

A system, consisting of elastic or absolutely rigid elements, linked by elastic connections, could be in a state of *stable* or *unstable* equilibrium, if system of static forces is applied. In the first case (first state), the application of infinitesimal perturbation, as infinitesimal displacements or increase of the load, to the system, deflects the system from its equilibrium.

The system restores its initial state for a finite time interval, when the perturbation is removed. If the equilibrium is unstable, the infinitesimal displacements or increase of the load lead to a significant increase of the deformations. *Stability of elastic systems* examines the methods of determining the static forces, under which a linear system transforms from stable into unstable equilibrium. In engineering the loss of stability is often called *buckling*.

The loads, under which a system transforms from stable into unstable equilibrium, are called: *buckling loads* or *buckling forces*.

Real systems contain infinite number of degrees of freedom. Nevertheless their behavior, regarding buckling, could be researched with a great precision by models with finite number of degrees of freedom.

The classical methods for determining the buckling forces are systemized in three types: *static*, *energy* and *dynamic* methods.

The *Static method* or equilibrium method is based on the equilibrium conditions of the systems. For a system with finite degrees of freedom, for instance, the buckling force is determinate by a system of linear equations. The *Energy method* uses the functional of the total potential energy of the system. The *Dynamic method* or also called kinematic method appears as the most universal method.

8.2 Euler buckling

We are going to obtain the Euler formulae for buckling of a rod with cross section A, supported in both ends, and loaded with an axial force F, *Figure 8.2*. In the same figure the coefficients μ are also shown.

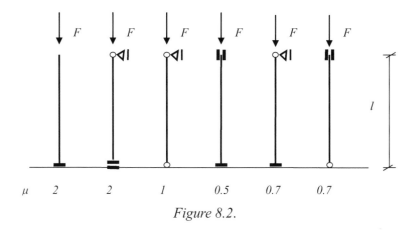

Figure 8.2.

If we denote by $w(x)$ the transverse displacement of the points of the rod, then the following differential equation is valid:

$$M(x) = EI_{min} \frac{d^2}{dx^2} w(x).$$ (8.1)

The bending moment for a cross section with coordinate x can be written as well as:

$$M(x) = Fw(x).$$ (8.2)

For a function, expressing the transverse displacement $w(x)$, we are going to use:

$$w(x) = A \sin kx + B \cos kx$$ (8.3)

where: $k = \sqrt{\dfrac{F}{EI_{min}}}$.

The boundary conditions for a rod, supported in both ends as shown in *Figure 8.2 (third case),* we could express as:

$$w(0)=0, \ w(l)=0, \ M(0)=0 \text{ и } M(l)=0. \qquad (8.4)$$

Coefficients A and B we obtain by:

$$w(0)= A\sin kx + B\cos kx = 0 \Rightarrow B = 0 \qquad (8.5.a)$$

and

$$w(l)= A\sin kl = 0. \qquad (8.5.b)$$

Here we have two possible cases. The first case corresponds to $A=0$, i.e. non-deformed rod. For arbitrary x, $w(x)=0$. The second case, i.e. $A \neq 0$, is valid if $\sin kl = 0$ and corresponds to infinite number of solutions, when $kl = n\pi$, for $n = 0,1,2,3,4,\ldots$.

If we assume, see eq. (8.3), that:

$$kl = \sqrt{\frac{F}{EI_{\min}}}l, \qquad (8.6)$$

we obtain:

$$F_n = \frac{(n\pi)^2 EI_{\min}}{l^2}, \qquad (8.7)$$

for $n = 1,2,3\ldots$.

In practice only the first value of n is of interest, i.e.:

$$F_1 = F_{cr} = \frac{\pi^2 EI_{\min}}{l^2}. \qquad (8.8)$$

Relation (8.8) is the Euler formulae for buckling force of a rod, supported in both ends as shown in *Figure 8.2 (third case)*.

If we use another type of supports, see *Figure 8.2*, we will obtain the general form of eq. (8.8), i.e.:

$$F_1 = F_{cr} = \frac{\pi^2 EI_{min}}{\mu^2 l^2},$$
(8.9)

where μ is a coefficient, depending on the type of supports. We are going to call it *buckling coefficient*.

The analysis of the above formulae shows that F_{cr} is directly proportional to the bending stiffness EI_{min} and inversely proportional to the second power of l. Besides that, it relates to the type of supports.

If $n = 1$ the deformed shapes of the rod are called *first buckling shape modes*, see *Figure 8.3*. First and second, i.e. for $n = 2$, buckling shape modes for the third case are illustrated in *Figure 8.4*.

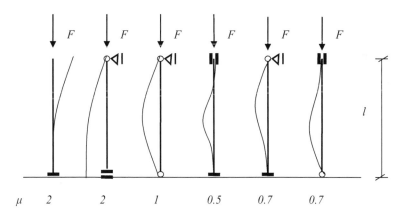

Figure 8.3. First buckling shape modes

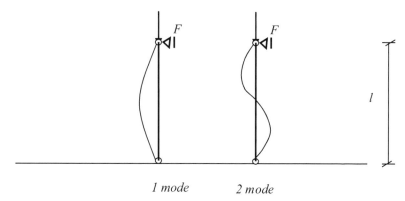

1 mode   *2 mode*

Figure 8.4. First and second buckling shape modes for third case

Euler formulae could be obtained as well by the *Method of initial parameters*. In accordance with this method, the values of quantities, for instance: $w(x)$, $\varphi(x)$, $M(x)$ or $Q(x)$, are expressed in a matrix form as:

$$\begin{Bmatrix} w(x) \\ \varphi(x) \\ M(x) \\ Q(x) \end{Bmatrix} = \begin{bmatrix} 1 & \dfrac{\sin kx}{k} & \dfrac{\cos kx - 1}{EIk^2} & \dfrac{\sin kx - kx}{EIk^3} \\ 0 & \cos kx & -\dfrac{\sin kx}{EIk} & \dfrac{\cos kx - 1}{EIk^2} \\ 0 & kEI\sin kx & \cos kx & \dfrac{\sin kx}{k} \\ 0 & 0 & 0 & 1 \end{bmatrix} \begin{Bmatrix} w_0 \\ \varphi_0 \\ M_0 \\ Q_0 \end{Bmatrix}$$

$$(8.10)$$

The initial parameters, the vector components in the right side of the matrix expression, are transformed into values, valid for a point with coordinate *x*, by matrix-operator called *transitional* matrix.

If we use this method for the third type of supports, see *Figure 8.2*, for a point with coordinate $x = l$ we obtain:

$$\begin{Bmatrix} w(l)=0 \\ \varphi(l) \\ M(l)=0 \\ Q(l)=0 \end{Bmatrix} = \begin{bmatrix} 1 & \dfrac{\sin kl}{k} & \dfrac{\cos kl-1}{EIk^2} & \dfrac{\sin kl-kl}{EIk^3} \\ 0 & \cos kl & -\dfrac{\sin kl}{EIk} & \dfrac{\cos kl-1}{EIk^2} \\ 0 & kEI\sin kl & \cos kl & \dfrac{\sin kl}{k} \\ 0 & 0 & 0 & 1 \end{bmatrix} \begin{Bmatrix} 0 \\ \varphi_0 \\ 0 \\ 0 \end{Bmatrix}$$

$$(8.11)$$

or for $w(l)$ we get:

$$w(l)=\begin{bmatrix} 1 & \dfrac{\sin kl}{k} & \dfrac{\cos kl-1}{EIk^2} & \dfrac{\sin kl-kl}{EIk^3} \end{bmatrix} \begin{Bmatrix} 0 \\ \varphi_0 \\ 0 \\ 0 \end{Bmatrix} = 0. \quad (8.12)$$

From (8.12) we obtain:

$$\frac{\sin kl}{k}\varphi_0 = 0. \qquad (8.13)$$

Because $\varphi_0 \neq 0$ then $\dfrac{\sin kl}{k} = 0$.

Here we have infinite number of solutions, when $kl = n\pi$, for $n = 0,1,2,3,4,\ldots$. Finally we obtain:

$$kl = n\pi = \sqrt{\frac{F}{EI_{min}}}\, l, \qquad (8.14)$$

or

$$F_n = \frac{(n\pi)^2 EI_{min}}{l^2}.$$ (8.15)

These expressions are identical with eqs. (8.6) and (8.7).

When we use another type of supports, i.e. boundary conditions of the rod, using (8.10) we could obtain the buckling force for each of the cases, shown in *Figure 8.2*.

8.3. Brief notes on the energy method

The Energy method is based on the functional of total virtual energy of the system. The expressions for the first and the second variations of the virtual energy are defined, and the first one equals to zero:

$$\delta\prod(q_1, q_2, q_3, ...) = 0,$$ (8.16)

where $q_1, q_2, q_3, ...$ are called *generalized* coordinates. In structural mechanics they could be identified with generalized displacements or displacements, in general. In this way the total virtual energy of the system characterizes the extremum of the functional, and the second variation shows the type of this extremum, respectively as:

$$\delta^2\prod(q_1, q_2, q_3, ...) < 0 \quad \text{maximum}$$ (8.17)

or

$$\delta^2\prod(q_1, q_2, q_3, ...) > 0 \quad \text{minimum}$$ (8.18)

Minimum of virtual energy is condition of stable equilibrium of the system.

Chapter **9**

Buckling of frame structures

Application of the force method and the displacement method in the buckling of frame structures

9.1. Application of the force method (flexibility method)

According to this method *released* (statically determinate) system must be chosen and *equations of compatibility*, in a form of system of linear equations, must be composed. If the applied load is only axial, then this system is homogeneous as:

$$[\delta]\{X\} = 0. \tag{9.1}$$

Symbolically, if the degree of statically indeterminacy is n, the flexibility matrix we express as:

$$[\delta] = \begin{bmatrix} \delta_{1,1} & \delta_{1,2} & \cdots & \delta_{1,n-1} & \delta_{1,n} \\ \delta_{2,1} & \delta_{2,2} & \cdots & \delta_{2,n-1} & \delta_{2,n} \\ \cdots & \cdots & \cdots & \cdots & \cdots \\ \delta_{n-1,1} & \delta_{n-1,2} & \cdots & \delta_{n-1,n-1} & \delta_{n-1,n} \\ \delta_{n,1} & \delta_{n,2} & \cdots & \delta_{n,n-1} & \delta_{n,n} \end{bmatrix}, \tag{9.2}$$

In contrast to already known application of the force method in analysis of statically indeterminate systems, here the coefficients δ_{ij} depend on the axial forces in compressed members. The obtained in this way displacements and internal forces are obviously higher in value. The increases of these quantities to be accounted, correctional functions are used.

Solutions of the correctional functions could be obtained from tables, calculated by corresponding to them relations. In these relations we introduce parameter, denoted as v.

Since the relation between flexibility matrix $[\delta]$ and stiffness matrix $[k]$ is:

$$[k]=[\delta]^{-1},\tag{9.3}$$

then the higher in value coefficients δ_{ij} correspond to lower in value stiffness coefficients. Different, i.e. modified through correctional functions, bending moment diagrams, used for computing of the coefficients δ_{ij}, allow the application of the force method in the buckling problems to be called *generalized*. Therefore, from now on, the generalized form of $[\delta]$ and $[k]$ we are going to denote respectively as $\left[\tilde{\delta}\right]$ and $\left[\tilde{k}\right]$.

The condition for neutrally stable equilibrium here, i.e. the occurrence of buckling or stability loss is:

$$\det\left|\tilde{\delta}\right|=0.\tag{9.4}$$

We can see that eq. (9.4) is the already known, equalization to zero of the determinant, using parameter. The parameter in this case is v, and is obtained from the relation:

$$v=kl=l\sqrt{\frac{N}{EI}}.\tag{9.5}$$

This parameter, on the other hand, is related to the axial load N. Solutions of eq. (9.4) are n values of v. From these values we could obtain the values of buckling (critical) axial loading. From practical interest is only the smallest value of v.

The problem is referred to obtaining these values of v, and from there, the values of N, for which the matrix $\left[\tilde{\delta}\right]$ becomes singular, i.e. the determinant of $\left[\tilde{\delta}\right]$ becomes zero.

9.2.   Application of the displacement method

The displacement method here is also called *generalized*. The coefficients of stiffness matrix are calculated by taking into account the axial forces, using correctional functions.

The condition for neutrally stable equilibrium in this method, i.e. occurrence of buckling or stability loss is:

$$\det\left|\tilde{k}\right| = 0 . \tag{9.6}$$

The interpretation of the matrix coefficients in matrix $\left[\tilde{k}\right]$, i.e. $\tilde{k}_{ij}$, is a nodal reaction at i due to unit displacement, applied at j, taking into account the axial loading. In contrast to already known application of the displacement method, here we use some correctional functions. We are going to express them as φ_i. As a whole, the matrix members (coefficients) in $\left[\tilde{k}\right]$ are smaller in value compared to the ones, known from the classical displacement method, studied in the discipline *Statics of indeterminate structures*.

The correctional functions can be obtained by applying the principle of virtual work. The final forms of these functions are:

$$\varphi_1(v) = \frac{v^2 \tan v}{3(\tan v - v)};$$

$$\varphi_2(v) = \frac{v}{8 \tan v} \frac{\tan v - v}{\left(\tan \dfrac{v}{2} - \dfrac{v}{2}\right)};$$

$$\varphi_3(v) = \frac{v}{4 \sin v} \frac{v - \sin v}{\left(\tan \dfrac{v}{2} - \dfrac{v}{2}\right)};$$

$$\varphi_4(v) = \frac{v^2}{12} \frac{\tan \dfrac{v}{2}}{\left(\tan \dfrac{v}{2} - \dfrac{v}{2}\right)};$$

$$\varphi_5(v) = \frac{v^3}{3(\tan v - v)};$$

$$\varphi_6(v) = \frac{v^3}{24\left(\tan \dfrac{v}{2} - \dfrac{v}{2}\right)} \quad \text{and}$$

$$\varphi_7(v) = v \tan v.$$

We see that the problem is referred to the already known equalization to zero of determinant, using parameter. This parameter, similarly to the application of the force method, derives from:

$$v = kl = l\sqrt{\frac{N}{EI}}. \tag{9.7}$$

Next is development of eq. (9.6), in a form of power polynomial, and obtaining the roots of its equalization to zero. Naturally, we are interested in this value of v, which corresponds, according to relation (9.7), to the smallest buckling axial force.

And here, the problem is referred to obtaining these values of v, and from there, the values of N, for which the matrix $\left[\tilde{k}\right]$ becomes singular, i.e. the determinant of $\left[\tilde{k}\right]$ becomes zero. This means that the condition for equilibrium:

$$\left[\tilde{k}\right]\{Z\} = 0 \tag{9.8}$$

is satisfied for a countless number of vectors $\{Z\}$. Typical and common for them is that the correlations between the components remain the same, and they describe the *buckling shape*.

The working stages, followed in the application of the displacement method in buckling problems, we are going to systematize into an algorithm:

- *Preliminary analysis of the system. Choice of method.*
- *Forming of restrained (kinematically determinate) system.*
- *Calculation of the coefficients of the stiffness matrix, using correctional functions in the axially compressed members.*
- *Obtaining of the parameters v_j for $j = 1, 2, 3, ..., n$, where n is the matrix size of (9.6). As we have already*

mentioned, for practical purposes we are interested in the smallest possible value of v, i.e. v_1.

- *Calculation of the buckling coefficients μ, and the smallest buckling value of the compress axial force N^{cr} for the individual members, and from there obtaining of the buckling (critical) external load F^{cr}.*
- *Obtaining of the effective buckling length of the members—l_i^{ef}.*
- *Computing of possible, indispensable reserve of loading capacity.*

Here we are going to show the relations, used in stages 5 and 6. For element *i* we have:

$$\mu_i = \pi / v_i$$

$$N_i^{cr} = \frac{v_i^2 EI}{l_i^2} = \frac{\pi_i^2 EI}{\left(\mu_i l_i\right)^2} = \frac{\pi_i^2 EI}{l_i^{ef\,2}},$$

where:

$$l_i^{ef} = \mu_i l_i.$$

Here the subscript of v shows to which element is related, and does not indicate root of eqs. (9.4) or (9.6), i.e. the subscript is connected with the relation (9.7).

The effective length of individual members, called also *buckling length,* could be adopted as a length of one entire semiwave, from the deformed shape of the member.

We can see that, the formulae, expressing the relation between N^{cr} and v_i or μ_i, is similar to the Euler formulae, from the previous chapter.

Chapter 10

Buckling of structures, modeled by one-dimensional finite elements. Geometrical stiffness matrix.

10.1. Introduction

Problems of buckling can be solved either through step-by-step increase of the loading or by finding the characteristic values of matrices. In the structural analysis these matrices are called *combined stiffness matrices,* and contain elastic parameters, geometrical dimensions of elements and a parameter, expressing axial forces.

The first approach, i.e. through increase of the loading, is more general by character, and could be used in non-linear systems. The second approach can only be used for linear systems. Based on this approach, the assumption that the load and the effects of it are proportional is used. For instance, in a case of double increase of the loading, we have double increase of the stresses.

10.1.1 Stiffness matrix.

In *Chapter 7* we have obtained the stiffness matrix and the equilibrium of beam element as:

$$[K_e] = \begin{bmatrix} \dfrac{EA}{l} & 0 & 0 & -\dfrac{EA}{l} & 0 & 0 \\[2mm] 0 & \dfrac{12EI}{l^3} & -\dfrac{6EI}{l^2} & 0 & -\dfrac{12EI}{l^3} & -\dfrac{6EI}{l^2} \\[2mm] 0 & -\dfrac{6EI}{l^2} & \dfrac{4EI}{l} & 0 & \dfrac{6EI}{l^2} & \dfrac{2EI}{l} \\[2mm] -\dfrac{EA}{l} & 0 & 0 & \dfrac{EA}{l} & 0 & 0 \\[2mm] 0 & -\dfrac{12EI}{l^3} & \dfrac{6EI}{l^2} & 0 & \dfrac{12EI}{l^3} & \dfrac{6EI}{l^2} \\[2mm] 0 & -\dfrac{6EI}{l^2} & \dfrac{2EI}{l} & 0 & \dfrac{6EI}{l^2} & \dfrac{4EI}{l} \end{bmatrix}.$$

$$(10.1)$$

$$\begin{bmatrix} \dfrac{EA}{l} & 0 & 0 & -\dfrac{EA}{l} & 0 & 0 \\[2mm] 0 & \dfrac{12EI}{l^3} & -\dfrac{6EI}{l^2} & 0 & -\dfrac{12EI}{l^3} & -\dfrac{6EI}{l^2} \\[2mm] 0 & -\dfrac{6EI}{l^2} & \dfrac{4EI}{l} & 0 & \dfrac{6EI}{l^2} & \dfrac{2EI}{l} \\[2mm] -\dfrac{EA}{l} & 0 & 0 & \dfrac{EA}{l} & 0 & 0 \\[2mm] 0 & -\dfrac{12EI}{l^3} & \dfrac{6EI}{l^2} & 0 & \dfrac{12EI}{l^3} & \dfrac{6EI}{l^2} \\[2mm] 0 & -\dfrac{6EI}{l^2} & \dfrac{2EI}{l} & 0 & \dfrac{6EI}{l^2} & \dfrac{4EI}{l} \end{bmatrix} \begin{Bmatrix} u_i \\ v_i \\ \varphi_i \\ u_j \\ v_j \\ \varphi_j \end{Bmatrix} = \begin{Bmatrix} F_i^x \\ F_i^y \\ M_i \\ F_j^x \\ F_j^y \\ M_j \end{Bmatrix}.$$

$$(10.2)$$

If the contribution of inertial and damping forces is significant (can not be ignored), the dynamic equilibrium, in matrix form, we express as:

$$[M_e]\{\ddot{u}_e\}+[C_e]\{\dot{u}_e\}+[K_e]\{u_e\}=\{F_e\}. \qquad (10.3)$$

10.1.2 Geometrical stiffness matrix.

Loading, close to the critical (buckling loading), significantly reduce the stiffness of structures. This effect can be taken into account by so called: *geometrical stiffness matrix,* denoted as $[K_e]^G$.

In this case, relation (10.3) we express as:

$$[M_e]\{\ddot{u}_e\}+[C_e]\{\dot{u}_e\}+[K_e]\{u_e\}-[K_e]^G\{u_e\}=\{F_e\}, \qquad (10.4)$$

where forces:

$$\{F_S\}^G=-[K_e]^G\{u_e\} \qquad (10.5)$$

are additional forces, due to change of the position and the axial forces in the elements.

Then the nodal dynamic equilibrium could be expressed as:

$$\{F_I\}+\{F_D\}+\{F_S\}-\{F_S\}^G=\{F^{ex}\}, \qquad (10.6)$$

where: $\{F_I\}$ - vector of inertial forces,

$\{F_D\}$ - vector of damping forces,

$\{F_S\}$ - vector of elastic forces,

$\{F_S\}^G$ - vector of additional forces, due to change of the position and the axial forces in the elements,

$\{F^{ex}\}$ - vector of external forces.

The coefficients in geometrical stiffness matrix depend on the axial loading. k_{ij}^G is a force, acting in direction of degree of freedom i, due to unit displacement in degree of freedom j, because of axial force effect.

10.1.3 Combined stiffness matrix.

Solution of (10.4), often expressed as

$$[M_e]\{\ddot{u}_e\}+[C_e]\{\dot{u}_e\}+\left[\tilde{K}_e\right]\{u_e\}=\{F_e\}, \qquad (10.7)$$

can be obtained by step-by-step increase of the loading. If inertial and damping forces are neglected, then we can write (10.4) as:

$$\left[\tilde{K}_e\right]\{u_e\}=\{F_e\}, \qquad (10.8)$$

where:

$$\left[\tilde{K}_e\right]=[K_e]-[K_e]^G, \qquad (10.9)$$

and is called *combined stiffness matrix.*

Let the beam element has four degrees of freedom, see *Chapter 7.* Then the stiffness matrix and geometrical stiffness matrix are:

$$[K_e]=\frac{EI}{l^3}\begin{bmatrix} 12 & 6l & -12 & 6l \\ 6l & 4l^2 & -6l & 2l^2 \\ -12 & -6l & 12 & -6l \\ 6l & 2l^2 & -6l & 4l^2 \end{bmatrix} \qquad (10.10)$$

and

$$[K_e]^G = \frac{N}{30l} \begin{bmatrix} 36 & 3l & -36 & 3l \\ 3l & 4l^2 & -3l & -l^2 \\ -36 & -3l & 36 & -3l \\ 3l & -l^2 & -3l & 4l^2 \end{bmatrix}. \tag{10.11}$$

We have mentioned that, problems of stability (buckling) of elastic systems could be solved through obtaining the characteristic values of matrices. They are values, which correspond to zeros of determinant. In this case, this is the determinant of *combined stiffness matrix*, shown through expression (10.9), but obtained from a system with suitably supported elements, i.e. $\left[\tilde{K} \right]$.

If we express (10.8) as $\left[\tilde{K} \right]\{u\} = \{F\} = 0$, i.e. for the entire system, and solve:

$$\det \left| \tilde{K} \right| = 0, \tag{10.12}$$

developing the left side in a form of power polynomial towards N, we will obtain n-values of N, solutions of eq. (10.12). Each root of (10.12) gives solution of $\left[\tilde{K} \right]\{u\} = \{F\}$ in $\{F\} = \{0\}$. As we already know, the smallest value of N represents the practical interest.

The equilibrium $\left[\tilde{K} \right]\{u\} = \{0\}$ is satisfied for n-vectors $\{u\}$. Every vector $\{u\}_i$ expresses the *i-th* buckling mode (shape). Relation (10.12) resembles (9.6) from the previous chapter. This approach is different than the increase of the loading.

10.2 Buckling of structures, modeled by large amount of degrees of freedom

Complex structures can be analyzed for buckling by computational models with large amount of degrees of freedom. In this case the matrix form (10.4) or (10.7) for the entire model, we express as:

$$[M]\{\ddot{u}\}+[C]\{\dot{u}\}+[K]\{u\}-[K]^{G}\{u\}=\{F\} \quad (10.13)$$

or

$$[M]\{\ddot{u}\}+[C]\{\dot{u}\}+[\tilde{K}]\{u\}=\{F\}. \quad (10.14)$$

Chapter **11**

Dynamics of structures. Single-degree of freedom system.

11.1   Introduction

Dynamics of elastic systems is a branch of *mechanics*, treating the dynamic equilibrium of elastic systems. The main subject of this discipline is: the methods, and in result, formation of computational models for adequate analysis of systems, taking into account the inertial and damping forces, due to the motion. *Dynamics of structures* is a branch of *structural mechanics*. The formulation of the computational models uses both, analytical or classical, and numerical methods.

11.2   Dynamics of linear elastic system

11.2.1 Computational models
In dynamics of elastic material systems we distinguish three basic types of computational models:

- *Single-degree of freedom systems (SDOF),*
- *Multi-degree of freedom systems (MDOF),*
- *Systems with infinite number of degrees of freedom.*

The first type includes the computational models of material systems, which response could be accurately described through one-degree of freedom, i.e. composing one equation of motion or equilibrium. Analogically, the systems with finite number of degrees of freedom, (MDOF), are computational models of material systems, which response could be described through finite number of degrees of freedom, i.e. through system of finite number of equations of motion. Systems with infinite number of degrees of freedom are models, where the mass is considered as continuous material characteristics.

With the term *degree of freedom* we will denote a *degree of freedom of mass point,* or often called *dynamic degree of freedom.*

11.3 Single-degree of freedom system

Let us examine the equilibrium of point m, treated as single-degree of freedom system, because only motion parallel to coordinate x is possible, *Figure 11.1.*

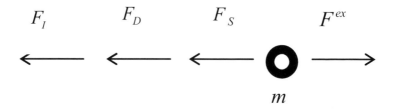

Figure 11.1. Dynamic equilibrium of point m.

The dynamic equilibrium of the point m we could express as:

$$F_I + F_D + F_S = F^{ex},$$ \qquad (11.1)

where:

$F_I = m\ddot{u}(t)$ is inertial force, due to the acceleration of the point m,

$F_D = c\dot{u}(t)$ - damping force, due to the damping property of the system,

$F_s = ku(t)$ - stiffness force,

$F^{ex} \equiv F(t)$ - external force.

After substituting the above equations in eq. (11.1) we obtain:

$$m\ddot{u}(t) + c\dot{u}(t) + ku(t) = F(t) = F^{ex}. \qquad (11.2)$$

Relation (11.2) expresses the dynamic equilibrium of the point m at time t, under the common action of inertial, damping, stiffness and external forces. Depending on which forces are taken into account in the equilibrium, we distinguish the following motions, called vibrations of the system:

- *free undamped vibrations,*
- *free damped vibrations,*
- *forced undamped vibrations,*
- *forced damped vibrations.*

11.3.1 Free undamped vibrations
In this case, we neglect the damping force and the external force at time t, which is already removed, i.e.:

$$F_D = c\dot{u}(t) = 0$$

and

$$F^{ex} \equiv F(t) = 0.$$

The dynamic equilibrium now, we express as:

$$m\ddot{u}(t) + ku(t) = 0 \qquad (11.3)$$

or

$$F_I + F_S = 0. \qquad (11.4)$$

The solution of such a type ordinarily homogeneous differential equation with constant coefficients, i.e. linear, see eq. (11.3), we could demand as:

$$u(t) = A\sin\omega t + B\cos\omega t, \qquad (11.5)$$

$$u(t) = C\sin(\omega t + \varphi) \qquad \text{or} \qquad (11.6)$$

$$u(t) = \overline{C}\exp(rt), \qquad (11.7)$$

where the constants A, B, C and $\overline{C}$ depend on the initial conditions of the motion. The notation φ means the so-called *initial phase* of the motion.

Substituting eq. (11.6) in eq. (11.3) and after differentiation we obtain:

$$m\ddot{u}(t) + ku(t) = -m\omega^2 u(t) + ku(t) = 0 \qquad (11.8)$$

or

$$-m\omega^2 C\sin(\omega t + \varphi) + kC\sin(\omega t + \varphi) = 0. \qquad (11.9)$$

Relation (11.9) we could write as:

$$-m\omega^2 C\cos(\omega t + \overline{\varphi}) + kC\cos(\omega t + \overline{\varphi}) = 0, \qquad (11.10)$$

where due to a change of the trigonometric function we have

$\overline{\varphi} = \varphi - \dfrac{\pi}{2}$. After rearranging the left side of eq. (11.10) we obtain:

$$\left[k - m\omega^2 \right] C \cos\left(\omega t + \overline{\varphi}\right) = 0 . \tag{11.11}$$

Equation (11.11) to be valid for every time t it is necessary to:

$$\left[k - m\omega^2 \right] = 0 \tag{11.12}$$

i.e.

$$\omega_1 = \omega_2 = \sqrt{\dfrac{k}{m}} \tag{11.13}$$

or

$$\omega = \sqrt{\dfrac{k}{m}} \quad \left[\dfrac{rad}{s} \right] . \tag{11.14}$$

The constant ω is called *circular frequency* or *angular velocity* of the free undamped vibrations. It expresses the number of vibrations per 2π seconds.

The natural frequency f, $[1/s]$, can be calculated by:

$$f = \dfrac{\omega}{2\pi} = \dfrac{1}{2\pi}\sqrt{\dfrac{k}{m}} \tag{11.16}$$

and expresses the number of vibrations of the material point per 1 second.

The natural period of the free undamped vibrations is:

$$T = \frac{1}{f} = \frac{2\pi}{\omega} \qquad (11.17)$$

and expresses the duration of one complete vibration cycle.

The constants C and $\overline{\phi}$ are obtained through relations:

$$C = \sqrt{u_0^2 + \frac{\dot{u}_0^2}{\omega^2}} \text{ and } \overline{\phi} = arctg \frac{u_0 \omega}{\dot{u}_0} - \frac{\pi}{2}, \qquad (11.18)$$

where: u_0 is initial displacement, and $\dot{u}_0$ - initial velocity.

Finally, we could express the motion as:

$$u(t) = \sqrt{u_0^2 + \frac{\dot{u}_0^2}{\omega^2}} \cos\left(\omega t + arctg \frac{u_0 \omega}{\dot{u}_0} - \frac{\pi}{2} \right). \qquad (11.19.a)$$

The motion depends on the inertial and stiffness characteristics of the system, i.e. m and k, see eq. (11.16).

If the solution we demand as in type of eq. (11.5), the coefficients A and B are, respectively $B = u_0$ and $A = \dot{u}_0 / \omega$. Here u_0 and $\dot{u}_0$ are: the initial displacement and the initial velocity. Then:

$$u(t) = A \sin \omega t + B \cos \omega t = \frac{\dot{u}_0}{\omega} \sin \omega t + u_0 \cos \omega t. \qquad (11.19.b)$$

11.3.2 Free damped vibrations

The differential equation of motion we express as:

$$m\ddot{u}(t) + c\dot{u}(t) + ku(t) = 0. \qquad (11.20.a)$$

If we assume that:

$\omega^2 = \dfrac{k}{m}$ and $\xi = \dfrac{c}{2m}$, eq. (11.20.a) transforms into:

$$\ddot{u}(t) + 2\xi\dot{u}(t) + \omega^2 u(t) = 0. \qquad (11.20.b)$$

Let us use the third type of the function $u(t)$, i.e. $u(t) = \bar{C}\exp(rt)$, see eq. (11.7). Then from eq. (11.20.b) we obtain:

$$r^2\bar{C}\exp(rt) + 2\xi r\bar{C}\exp(rt) + \omega^2\bar{C}\exp(rt) = 0 \qquad (11.21)$$

or

$$\left(r^2 + 2\xi r + \omega^2\right)\bar{C}\exp(rt) = 0. \qquad (11.22)$$

The problem reduces to solving the following characteristic equation:

$$r^2 + 2\xi r + \omega^2 = 0, \qquad (11.23)$$

the roots of which we obtain from:

$$r_{1,2} = -\xi \pm \sqrt{\xi^2 - \omega^2}. \qquad (11.24)$$

Depending on the sign of the radical $R = \xi^2 - \omega^2$, we distinguish three cases:

- $R = \xi^2 - \omega^2 > 0$, i.e. $|\xi| > |\omega|$ or $\omega < \dfrac{c}{2m}$, where $c > c_{cr}$,

- $R = \xi^2 - \omega^2 = 0$, i.e. $|\xi| = |\omega|$ or $\omega = \dfrac{c}{2m}$, where $c = c_{cr}$ and

- $R = \xi^2 - \omega^2 < 0$, i.e. $|\xi| < |\omega|$ or $\omega > \dfrac{c}{2m}$, where $c < c_{cr}$, in which $c_{cr} = 2m\omega$ is called *critical damping*. Important for the civil structures is the third case. There are no vibrations if $c \geq c_{cr}$.

The solution of eq. (11.20.a) now we express as:

$$u(t) = C\sin(\omega_D t + \varphi_D)\exp(-\tilde{\xi}t) \qquad (11.25)$$

or

$$u(t) = (A\sin(\omega_D t) + B\cos(\omega_D t))\exp(-\tilde{\xi}t), \qquad (11.26)$$

where:

$$\omega_D = \omega\sqrt{1-\xi^2} \text{ и } \tilde{\xi} \equiv r. \qquad (11.27.a)$$

We could obtain the period of free damped vibrations from:

$$T_D = \frac{2\pi}{\omega_D} = 2\pi / \omega\sqrt{1-\xi^2}. \qquad (11.27.b)$$

11.3.3 Forced undamped vibrations. Forced undamped vibrations from harmonic load

The equilibrium equation, or called also differential equation of motion in this case, is obtained from eq. (11.2), considering that:

$$F_D = c\dot{u}(t) = 0$$

and

$$F^{ex} \equiv F(t) \neq 0,$$

we express as:

$$m\ddot{u}(t) + ku(t) = F(t). \tag{11.28}$$

The forced undamped vibrations could be caused from: periodical, particularly harmonic, impulse or arbitrary loads or disturbances. In *figure 11.2* is shown a time-variable harmonic load. Main characteristics are: amplitude, period and frequency.

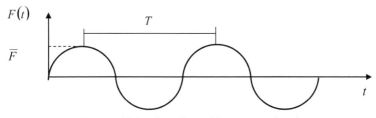

Figure 11.2: Graphic of harmonic load.

Let us assume that the load is harmonic, from type:

$$F^{ex} \equiv F(t) = \overline{F}\sin(\theta t + \varphi_\theta) \tag{11.29}$$

or

$$F^{ex} \equiv F(t) = \overline{F}\cos(\theta t + \overline{\varphi}_\theta). \tag{11.30}$$

After we substitute eq. (11.29) in eq. (11.28), we obtain:

$$m\ddot{u}(t) + ku(t) = \overline{F}\sin(\theta t + \varphi_\theta). \tag{11.31}$$

This is non-homogeneous, second order ordinary differential equation, with constant coefficients, i.e. linear. Its total solution is a sum of: the solution of homogeneous equation (11.3) and a partial solution of eq. (11.31). We will express this as:

$$u(t) = u^C(t) + u^P(t). \tag{11.32}$$

We have already obtained the solution $u^C(t)$ of the homogeneous equation (11.3), see eq. (11.19). For the partial solution, we are searching as:

$$u^P(t) = U \sin(\theta t + \varphi_\theta), \tag{11.33}$$

and we obtain:

$$u^P(t) = \frac{\overline{F}}{k} \frac{1}{1-\eta^2} \sin(\theta t + \varphi_\theta) = \mu u^{st} \sin(\theta t + \varphi_\theta), \tag{11.34}$$

where: $U = \dfrac{\overline{F}}{k} \dfrac{1}{1-\eta^2}$, $\dfrac{\overline{F}}{k} = u^{st}$ is the displacement of the mass point from static action of force $\overline{F}$, $\mu = \dfrac{1}{1-\eta^2}$ is called *dynamic coefficient*, and $\eta = \dfrac{\theta}{\omega}$.

For the total solution of eq. (11.31) we obtain:

$$u(t) = u^C(t) + u^P(t) = C \sin(\omega t + \varphi) + \frac{\overline{F}}{k} \frac{1}{1-\eta^2} \sin(\theta t + \varphi_\theta) \tag{11.35.a}$$

or

$$u(t) = u^C(t) + u^P(t) = C \sin(\omega t + \varphi) + u^{st} \mu \sin(\theta t + \varphi_\theta). \tag{11.36.a}$$

Substituting eq. (11.19) in eq. (11.35.a) and eq. (11.36.a), we obtain:

$$u(t) = \sqrt{u_0^2 + \frac{\dot{u}_0^2}{\omega^2}} \cos\left(\omega t + arctg\,\frac{u_0\omega}{\dot{u}_0} - \frac{\pi}{2}\right) + \frac{\overline{F}}{k}\frac{1}{1-\eta^2}\sin\left(\theta t + \varphi_\theta\right)$$

(11.35.b)

or

$$u(t) = \sqrt{u_0^2 + \frac{\dot{u}_0^2}{\omega^2}} \cos\left(\omega t + arctg\,\frac{u_0\omega}{\dot{u}_0} - \frac{\pi}{2}\right) + u^{st}\mu\sin\left(\theta t + \varphi_\theta\right).$$

(11.36.b)

Here again has been used the relation $\overline{\varphi} = \varphi - \dfrac{\pi}{2}$.

Analyzing the above relations, i.e. eq. (11.35.b) and eq. (11.36.b), we are going to conclude that the motion is a sum of: the motion, due to external load, and the one, due to initial conditions, for instance, initial velocity or initial displacement.

In this way, for one-degree of freedom system, the equation of motion we could express as:

$$u(t) = -d_{11}m\ddot{u}(t) + \Delta_{1F}\sin\theta t,$$

(11.38.c)

where $d_{11}m\ddot{u}(t)$ is the displacement at moment t, due to inertial force $m\ddot{u}(t)$; $\Delta_{1F}\sin\theta t$ is a displacement due to the external force, again at moment t. The notations d_{11} and Δ_{1F} are known from the method of elastic displacements. Let us assume that, the motion could be expressed as harmonic, from type:

$$u(t) = U\sin\theta t,$$

(11.38.d)

where U is the amplitude value of the displacement.

Then, from eq. (11.38.c) we obtain:

$$U \sin \theta t = d_{11} \theta^2 mU \sin \theta t + \Delta_{1F} \sin \theta t. \qquad (11.38.e)$$

Since we are interested in the maximum in value displacements, we assume that $\sin \theta t = 1$. Then:

$$U = d_{11} \theta^2 mU + \Delta_{1F} \qquad (11.38.f)$$

or

$$\left(d_{11} \theta^2 m - 1 \right) U + \Delta_{1F} = 0 \qquad (11.38.g)$$

and

$$\left(d_{11} - \frac{1}{\theta^2 m} \right) \theta^2 mU + \Delta_{1F} = 0. \qquad (11.38.h)$$

The above relation contains the multiplier $\theta^2 mU$, which is assumed to be the maximum value of the inertial force, i.e. $F_I^{\max} = \theta^2 mU$.

Finally, we will denote that:

$$\left(d_{11} - \frac{1}{\theta^2 m} \right) F_I^{\max} + \Delta_{1F} = 0. \qquad (11.38.i)$$

For the maximum bending moments we use the superposition expressed as:

$$M^{dyn} = M_{F_I=1}^{d} F_I^{\max} + M_{\bar{F}}^{d}.$$

Here M^{dyn} contains the maximum values of the bending moments, and we are going to call it *dynamic momentum diagram*, where $M_{F_I=1}^d$ and $M_{\overline{F}}^d$ are diagrams, respectively from the forces $F_I = 1kN$ and $\overline{F}$.

11.3.4 Forced damped vibrations

The equilibrium equation or called also differential equation of motion in this case, in *forced damped vibrations*, is:

$$m\ddot{u}(t) + c\dot{u}(t) + ku(t) = F(t). \tag{11.39}$$

If we assume again that:

$$\omega^2 = \frac{k}{m} \text{ and } \xi = \frac{c}{2m}, \text{ equation (11.39) transforms as:}$$

$$\ddot{u}(t) + 2\xi\dot{u}(t) + \omega^2 u(t) = \frac{1}{m}F(t). \tag{11.40}$$

11.3.5 Resonance

A condition of resonance occurs when:

$$\eta = \frac{\theta}{\omega} = 1, \tag{11.41}$$

and the dynamic coefficient towards infinity, i.e.:

$$\mu = \frac{1}{1-\eta^2} \to \infty. \tag{11.42}$$

We are not going to review this condition in details, despite its importance, because it has been widely researched in the literature.

11.3.6 Response of single-degree of freedom system, described by the Duhamel integral

The displacement of single-degree of freedom system at time t, due to arbitrary load can be expressed by the Duhamel integral as:

$$u(t) = \frac{1}{m\omega} \int_0^t f(\bar{\tau}) \sin \omega (t - \bar{\tau}) d\bar{\tau} \qquad (11.43)$$

then the total displacement (total response) is:

$$u^t(t) = \frac{\dot{u}(0)}{\omega} \cos(\omega t) + u(0)\sin(\omega t) + \frac{1}{m\omega} \int_0^t f(\bar{\tau}) \sin \omega (t - \bar{\tau}) d\bar{\tau} \cdot \qquad (11.44)$$

If the damping is taken into account eq. (11.44) becomes:

$$u^t(t) = \left[\frac{\dot{u}(0) + u(0)\tilde{\xi}}{\omega_D} \cos(\omega_D t) + u(0)\sin(\omega_D t) \right] \exp(-\tilde{\xi}t) +$$

$$+ \frac{1}{m\omega_D} \int_0^t f(\bar{\tau}) \sin \omega_D (t - \bar{\tau}) \exp - \xi\omega(t - \bar{\tau}) d\bar{\tau} \qquad (11.45)$$

or

$$u^t(t) = \sqrt{u_0^2 + \frac{\dot{u}_0^2}{\omega_D^2}} \sin\left(\omega_D t + arctg \frac{u_0 \omega_D}{\dot{u}_0} \right) \exp(-\tilde{\xi}t) +$$

$$+ \frac{1}{m\omega_D} \int_0^t f(\bar{\tau}) \sin \omega_D (t - \bar{\tau}) \exp - \xi\omega(t - \bar{\tau}) d\bar{\tau} \qquad , (11.46)$$

where ω_D is called *damping circular frequency*.

We are going to see in the next two chapters, that the dynamic response of real systems depends on the mass and stiffness distribution through the so-called shape functions. And something more, we can provoke the more desirable dynamic response by "reordering" the sequence of the shape functions.

11.4 Dynamic loads

In *Figure 11.3 harmonic, periodic, impulse* and *arbitrary* loads are shown:

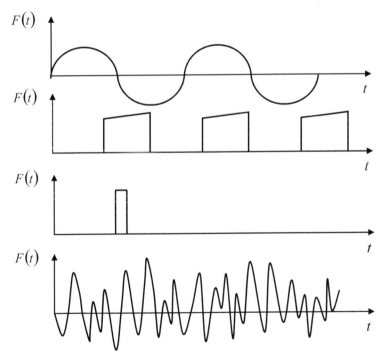

Figure 11.3 Harmonic, periodic, impulse and *arbitrary* loads.

Chapter **12**

Multi-degree of freedom systems

12.1 Multi-degree of freedom systems, analysed by equations of motion

12.1.1 Free vibrations (free undamped vibrations)

The equation of motion of *i-th* degree of freedom of system with *n* degrees of freedom, called also "d" form, could be expressed as:

$$\sum_{j=1}^{n} \delta_{ij} m_j \ddot{u}_j + u_i = 0 , \qquad (12.1)$$

where δ_{ij} is the displacement in *i-th* degree of freedom, due to unit force in direction of *j-th* degree of freedom,

m_j - concentrated mass in direction of *j-th* degree of freedom,

$\ddot{u}_j$ - acceleration in direction of *j-th* degree of freedom,

u_i - displacement in direction of *i-th* degree of freedom.

The coefficients δ_{ij} can be calculated by diagrams of internal forces.

In matrix form, regarding all n degrees of freedom, the equations of motions are:

$$[\delta][m]\{\ddot{u}\} + \{u\} = 0 . \tag{12.2}$$

If we assume harmonic type of motion:

$$\{\ddot{u}\} = -\omega^2 \{u\}, \tag{12.3}$$

and using (12.2) we obtain:

$$-\omega^2 [\delta][m]\{u\} + \{u\} = 0 \tag{12.4}$$

or

$$\left[-\omega^2 [\delta][m] + [I] \right] \{u\} = 0 . \tag{12.5}$$

To obtain non-trivial solution of (12.5), it's nessecery that:

$$\det \left| -\omega^2 [\delta][m] + [I] \right| = 0 . \tag{12.6}$$

As a result we obtain a polynomial of n-power with respect to ω^2, and we have n numbers, which are roots of (12.6).

Arranged in ascending order in vector:

$$\{\omega\}^T = \{\omega_1 \omega_2 \omega_3 ... \omega_n\}, \tag{12.7}$$

form the so-called *frequency vector* of the system.

Each natural frequency ω_i has a corresponding vector $\{\phi_i\}$, which we are going to call *eigenvector* or *modal vector.* Such a vector gives information about the proportions between the components of the displacements.

If we now substitute ω_i^2 in (12.5) and assume that, for instance $u_i^k = 1$, we could obtain the other components of the eigenvector. This procedure is called *normalization* and often $u_1^k = 1$ is choosen.

The eigenvector characterizes the vibration of the system with frequency, corresponding to the vector, for instance *i-th*:

$$\{\phi_i\}^T = \{\phi_i^1 \phi_i^2 \phi_i^3 ... \phi_i^n\}. \tag{12.8}$$

These vectors are orthogonal each other, i.e.:

$$\{\phi_i\}^T [m]\{\phi_j\} = 0 \tag{12.9}$$

or

$$\{\phi_i\}^T [k]\{\phi_j\} = 0. \tag{12.10}$$

12.1.2 Forced vibrations (forced undamped harmonic vibrations)

In this case eq. (12.1) we express as:

$$\sum_{j=1}^{n} \delta_{ij} m_j \ddot{u}_j + u_i = \sum_{k=1}^{m} \delta_{ik} F_k, \tag{12.11.a}$$

where $\delta_{ik} F_k$ is displacement of *i-th* mass (point *i*) due to external force F_k (applied at point *k*).

Then the forced vibrations can be described by the differential equations of motion, expressed in a matrix form as:

$$[\delta][m]\{\ddot{u}\} + \{u\} = \{\Delta_F\}. \tag{12.11.b}$$

Taking into account that:

$$\{\ddot{u}\} = -\theta^2 \{u\}, \tag{12.12}$$

from eq. (12.11.b) we obtain:

$$-\theta^2 [\delta][m]\{u\} + \{u\} = \{\Delta_F\} \tag{12.13}$$

or

$$\left[[I] - \theta^2 [\delta][m]\right]\{u\} = \{\Delta_F\}. \tag{12.14}$$

Here $\{u\}$ is vector of the dynamic displacements of the masses, i.e. total displacements.

In the interval of so-called *established vibrations* from harmonic load, i.e. no vibrations, due to initial displacements and velocities, we have:

$$\{u\} = \{u_0\}\sin(\theta t + \varphi_\theta), \tag{12.15}$$

where:

$$\{u_0\}^T = \{u_0^1 u_0^2 u_0^3 ... u_0^n\}, \tag{12.16}$$

is vector of the amplitude values of the displacements.

In the interval of so-called *unestablished vibrations*, the vector of the displacements $\{u\}$ is expressed as:

$$\{u\} = \{u\}^c + \{u\}^p, \tag{12.17}$$

where:

$\{u\}^c$ is vector of displacements, due to free vibrations, and is a solution of the homogenous system (12.2),

$\{u\}^p$ is vector of displacements, due to the external harmonic load, and is a solution of the non-homogenous system (12.11.b).

The total solution now, we express as:

$$\{u\} = \{u\}^c + \{u\}^p = \{U\}\sin(\omega t + \varphi) + \{u\}^p, \qquad (12.18)$$

where $\{U\}$ is vector of the amplitude values of the displacements.

If the external loads are described by harmonic functions as:

$$\{F(t)\} = \{\overline{F}\}\sin(\theta t + \varphi_\theta), \qquad (12.19)$$

where:

$$\{\overline{F}\}^T = \{\overline{F}_0^1 \overline{F}_0^2 \overline{F}_0^3 ... \overline{F}_0^n\}, \qquad (12.20)$$

is vector of amplitude values of the forces, the total displacements are:

$$\{u\} = \{u\}^c + \{u\}^p = \{U\sin(\omega t + \varphi)\} + \left\{\frac{\overline{F}}{k}\frac{1}{1-\eta^2}\right\}\sin(\theta t + \varphi_\theta) \qquad (12.21)$$

or

$$\{u\} = \{u\}^c + \{u\}^p = \{U^1\sin\omega t\} + \{U^2\cos\omega t\} + \left\{\frac{\overline{F}}{k}\frac{1}{1-\eta^2}\right\}\sin(\theta t + \varphi_\theta). \qquad (12.22)$$

Here $\eta_i = \dfrac{\theta}{\omega_i}$. (12.23)

12.1.3 Two-degree of freedom systems

In this case, the equations of motion, related to free undamped vibrations, could be expressed as:

$$\begin{bmatrix} \left(\bar{d}_{11} - \chi_\omega^d \dfrac{m_c}{m_1}\right) & \bar{d}_{12} \\ \bar{d}_{21} & \left(\bar{d}_{22} - \chi_\omega^d \dfrac{m_c}{m_2}\right) \end{bmatrix} \begin{Bmatrix} S_1 \\ S_2 \end{Bmatrix} = 0, \qquad (12.24)$$

where $\bar{d}_{ij}$ are standard displacements due to unit forces, obtained from expressions $\bar{d}_{ij} = d_{ij} EI_C$ (d_{ij} are identical with δ_{ij}), $\chi_\omega^d = \dfrac{EI_C}{m_C \omega^2}$, $S_i = m_i \omega^2 u_i$, and m_c is assumed as referred mass.

If we denote:

$$[\bar{D}] = \begin{bmatrix} \left(\bar{d}_{11} - \chi_\omega^d \dfrac{m_c}{m_1}\right) & \bar{d}_{12} \\ \bar{d}_{21} & \left(\bar{d}_{22} - \chi_\omega^d \dfrac{m_c}{m_2}\right) \end{bmatrix}, \qquad (12.25)$$

we need to calculate the roots of:

$$\det[\bar{D}] = \det \begin{bmatrix} \left(\bar{d}_{11} - \chi_\omega^d \dfrac{m_c}{m_1}\right) & \bar{d}_{12} \\ \bar{d}_{21} & \left(\bar{d}_{22} - \chi_\omega^d \dfrac{m_c}{m_2}\right) \end{bmatrix} = 0, (12.26)$$

which we express as: $\chi_{\omega 1}^d$ и $\chi_{\omega 2}^d$ ($\chi_{\omega 1}^d > \chi_{\omega 2}^d$).

Then, using the relations:

$$\omega_1 = \sqrt{\frac{EI_C}{m_C \chi_{\omega 1}^d}} \quad \text{and} \quad \omega_2 = \sqrt{\frac{EI_C}{m_C \chi_{\omega 2}^d}}, \qquad (12.27)$$

we obtain the eigenvalues, and through them—the eigenvectors:

$$\{\phi_1\}^T = \{\phi_1^1 \phi_1^2\} \quad \text{and} \quad \{\phi_2\}^T = \{\phi_2^1 \phi_2^2\} \qquad (12.28)$$

or

$$\{\phi_1\}^T = \{1 \phi_1^2\} \quad \text{and} \quad \{\phi_2\}^T = \{1 \phi_2^2\}. \qquad (12.29)$$

Relations (12.11) denote that, the displacement is a sum of: displacements, due to inertial forces, and due to external loads. Then, the dynamic bending moment diagrams could be obtained from:

$$M_{dyn} = M_{st}^{\bar{F}} + M_{S1=1}S_1 + M_{S2=1}S_2, \qquad (12.30)$$

where $M_{st}^{\bar{F}}$, $M_{S1=1}$ and $M_{S2=1}$ are respectively: a bending moment diagram due to static application of the amplitude values of the forces, a bending moment diagram due to unit force, applied in direction of the vibration of the first mass, and a bending moment diagram due to unit force, applied in direction of the vibration of the second mass. Here S_1 and S_2 are inertial forces, applied in directions of vibration of the masses, due to the external loads. These forces can be obtained from:

$$\begin{bmatrix} \left(\bar{d}_{11} - \chi_0^d \dfrac{m_c}{m_1}\right) & \bar{d}_{12} \\ \bar{d}_{21} & \left(\bar{d}_{22} - \chi_0^d \dfrac{m_c}{m_2}\right) \end{bmatrix} \begin{Bmatrix} S_1 \\ S_2 \end{Bmatrix} = \begin{bmatrix} \bar{d}_{11}^* & \bar{d}_{12} \\ \bar{d}_{21}^* & \bar{d}_{22}^* \end{bmatrix} \begin{Bmatrix} S_1 \\ S_2 \end{Bmatrix} = \begin{Bmatrix} \Delta_{1F} \\ \Delta_{2F} \end{Bmatrix}.$$

The total displacements, due to these forces can be illustrated as, see *figure 12.1*.

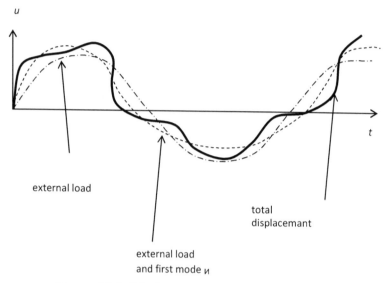

external load

external load
and first mode и

total
displacemant

Figure 12.1: Displacement at a point of the model.

12.2 Multi-degree of freedom systems, analysed by equilibrium equations

12.2.1 Free vibrations

The equilibrium equation in the direction of *i-th* degree of freedom of system with *n* degrees of freedom, is:

$$m_i \ddot{u}_i + \sum_{j=1}^{n} k_{ij} u_j = 0, \qquad (12.31)$$

where k_{ij} is force, acting in the *i-th* degree of freedom due to unit displacement in *j-th* degree of freedom,

m_i - concentrated mass in direction of *i-th* degree of freedom,

$\ddot{u}_i$ - acceleration in direction of *i-th* degree of freedom,

u_j - displacement in direction of *j-th* degree of freedom.

Relation (12.31) is also called "*k*" form of the equation of motion or *dynamic equilibrium equation* and expresses the dynamic equilibrium in the direction of *i-th* degree of freedom.

In matrix form for *n* degrees of freedom we have:

$$[m]\{\ddot{u}\} + [k]\{u\} = 0. \tag{12.32}$$

If we take into account that:

$$\{\ddot{u}\} = -\omega^2 \{u\} \tag{12.33}$$

from (12.32) we obtain:

$$-\omega^2 [m]\{u\} + [k]\{u\} = 0 \tag{12.34}$$

or

$$\left[-\omega^2 [m] + [k] \right] \{u\} = 0. \tag{12.35}$$

To obtain non-trivial solution, it's nessecery:

$$\det \left| [k] - \omega^2 [m] \right| = 0. \tag{12.36}$$

As a result we obtain a polynomial of *n*-power with respect to ω^2, and we have *n* numbers, which are roots of (12.36). Arranged in ascending order, i.e as:

$$\{\omega\}^T = \{\omega_1 \omega_2 \omega_3 ... \omega_n\} \tag{12.37}$$

are called *frequency vector* of the system.

The next step is: to obtain the components of the corresponding eigenvectors. And here, these vectors could be expressed as:

$$\{\phi_i\}^T = \{\phi_i^1 \phi_i^2 \phi_i^3 ... \phi_i^n\}. \tag{12.38}$$

If the both sides of eq. (12.32) we multiply on the left with $[d]$, and take into consideration that:

$$[d]^{-1} = [k], \quad \text{т.e} \quad [d][k] = [I] \tag{12.39}$$

we obtain:

$$[d][m]\{\ddot{u}\} + [d][k]\{u\} = 0 \tag{12.40}$$

or

$$[d][m]\{\ddot{u}\} + [I]\{u\} = [d][m]\{\ddot{u}\} + \{u\} = 0, \tag{12.41}$$

which represents the equations of motion in "*d*" form.

12.2.2 Forced harmonic vibrations

The forced vibrations could be described by the following equations of motion:

$$[m]\{\ddot{u}\} + [k]\{u\} = \{F(t)\}. \tag{12.42}$$

If the loads are harmonic, and could be expressed as:

$$\{F(t)\} = \{\bar{F}\}\sin(\theta t + \varphi_\theta), \tag{12.43}$$

where:

$$\{\bar{F}\}^{T} = \{\bar{F}_{1}\bar{F}_{2}\bar{F}_{3}...\bar{F}_{n}\}, \qquad (12.44)$$

is vector of the amplitude values of the forces. Then considering that:

$$\{\ddot{u}\} = -\theta^{2} \{u\}, \qquad (12.45)$$

we could express (12.42) as:

$$-\theta^{2} [m]\{u\} + [k]\{u\} = \{\bar{F}\}\sin(\theta t + \varphi_{\theta}) \qquad (12.46)$$

or

$$\left[[k] - \theta^{2} [m]\right]\{u\} = \{\bar{F}\}\sin(\theta t + \varphi_{\theta}). \qquad (12.47)$$

The vector of the established vibrations of the system is:

$$\{u\} = \{u_{0}\}\sin(\theta t + \varphi_{\theta}), \qquad (12.48)$$

In the interval of non-established vibrations, the vector $\{u\}$ could be decompossed as:

$$\{u\} = \{u\}^{c} + \{u\}^{p}, \qquad (12.49)$$

where:

$\{u\}^{c}$ is vector of displacements, due to free vibrations and it's a solution of the homogenous system (12.32), and

$\{u\}^{p}$ is vector of displacements, due to the external harmonic load and it's a solution of (12.42).

The total solution is:

$$\{u\} = \{u\}^c + \{u\}^p = \{U\}\sin(\omega t + \varphi) + \{u\}^p, \qquad (12.50)$$

where $\{U\}$ contains the amplitude values of displacements.
If the external loads are expressed as:

$$\{F(t)\} = \{\overline{F}\}\sin(\theta t + \varphi_\theta), \qquad (12.51)$$

where:

$$\{\overline{F}\}^T = \{\overline{F}_0^1 \overline{F}_0^2 \overline{F}_0^3 ... \overline{F}_0^n\}, \qquad (12.52)$$

is vector of the amplitude values of forces, then:

$$\{u\} = \{u\}^c + \{u\}^p = \{U\sin(\omega t + \varphi)\} + \left\{\frac{\overline{F}}{k}\frac{1}{1-\eta^2}\right\}\sin(\theta t + \varphi_\theta)$$
$$(12.53)$$

or

$$\{u\} = \{u\}^c + \{u\}^p = \{U^1\sin\omega t\} + \{U^2\cos\omega t\} + \left\{\frac{\overline{F}}{k}\frac{1}{1-\eta^2}\right\}\sin(\theta t + \varphi_\theta)$$
$$(12.54)$$

There is an equivalency between the both forms of the equations, equations of motion and equilibrium equations.

12.1.3 Two-degree of freedom sysrems
The dynamic equilibrium equations could be expressed as:

$$\left[\begin{matrix} \left(\overline{k}_{11} - \chi_{\omega}^{k} \dfrac{m_1}{m_c} \right) & \overline{k}_{12} \\[2ex] \overline{k}_{21} & \left(\overline{k}_{22} - \chi_{\omega}^{k} \dfrac{m_2}{m_c} \right) \end{matrix}\right] \left\{\begin{matrix} U_1 \\ U_2 \end{matrix}\right\} = 0, \qquad (12.55)$$

where: $\overline{k}_{ij} = \dfrac{k_{ij}}{EI_c}$ is force in node i, due to unit displacement in node j, divided by $1/EI_c$. With χ_{ω}^{k} is denoted $\dfrac{m_c \omega^2}{EI_c}$, i.e. $\chi_{\omega}^{k} = \dfrac{m_c \omega^2}{EI_c}$, and by m_c—assumed as referred mass. Obviously: $\chi_{\omega}^{k} = \left(\chi_{\omega}^{d} \right)^{-1}$.

If we use:

$$[\overline{K}] = \left[\begin{matrix} \left(\overline{k}_{11} - \chi_{\omega}^{k} \dfrac{m_1}{m_c} \right) & \overline{k}_{12} \\[2ex] \overline{k}_{21} & \left(\overline{k}_{22} - \chi_{\omega}^{k} \dfrac{m_2}{m_c} \right) \end{matrix}\right], \qquad (12.56)$$

then we need to calculate the roots of:

$$\det[\overline{K}] = \det \left[\begin{matrix} \left(\overline{k}_{11} - \chi_{\omega}^{k} \dfrac{m_1}{m_c} \right) & \overline{k}_{12} \\[2ex] \overline{k}_{21} & \left(\overline{k}_{22} - \chi_{\omega}^{k} \dfrac{m_2}{m_c} \right) \end{matrix}\right] = 0, \qquad (12.57)$$

which we express as: $\chi_{\omega 1}^{k}$ and $\chi_{\omega 2}^{k}$. Taking into consideration that $\chi_{\omega 1}^{k} > \chi_{\omega 2}^{k}$, and using the relations:

$$\omega_1 = \sqrt{\frac{EI_C \chi_{\omega 2}^k}{m_C}} \quad \text{и} \quad \omega_2 = \sqrt{\frac{EI_C \chi_{\omega 1}^k}{m_C}}, \qquad (12.58)$$

we could obtain the eigenvalues, and through them—the eigenvectors of the system.

The dynamic bending moment diagram could be expressed by:

$$M_{dyn} = M_{st}^{\bar{F}} + M_{U1=1}U_1 + M_{U2=1}U_2, \qquad (12.59)$$

where $M_{st}^{\bar{F}}$, $M_{U1=1}$ и $M_{U2=1}$ are respectively: bending moments due to static application of the amplitude values of the forces, bending moments due to unit displacement in direction of vibration of the first mass, bending moments due to unit displacement in direction of vibration of the second mass, valid for the restrained system. Here U_1 and U_2 are displacements in directions of vibration of the masses. In the obtained in this way diagrams $M_{st}^{\bar{F}}$, $M_{U1=1}$ and $M_{U2=1}$ can be treated as a basis, U_1 and U_2—weight coefficients.

Chapter **13**

Systems with large number of degrees of freedom

13.1 Dynamic analysis of multi-degree of freedom systems.

In *Chapter 12* we have discussed two methods of dynamic analysis of multi-degree of freedom systems. These methods we have called:

- *Dynamic analysis of multi-degree of freedom systems, analysed by equations of motion;*
- *Dynamic analysis of multi-degree of freedom systems, analysed by equilibrium equations.*

However, they have a limited application, because of the fact that they ignore the damping forces, and the external forces are assumed as harmonic.

13.1.1 Modal analysis

Differential equations of motion in the case of free undamped vibrations of multi-degree of freedom system are composed in a completely analogical form as those, related to systems with small number of degrees of freedom. In FEM matrix form we have:

$$[m]\{\ddot{u}\}+[k]\{u\}=0, \tag{13.1}$$

where matrices $[m]$ and $[k]$ are squire symmetrical matrices, with dimensions equal to the number of the selected degrees of freedom of the system, called respectively mass matrix and stiffness matrix. The vectors $\{\ddot{u}\}$ and $\{u\}$ are called respectively *nodal accelerations vector* and *nodal displacements vector*.

This type of analysis in program systems, i.e. calculation of natural frequencies and modes of vibrations, is called *modal analysis* or *vibration analysis*. By nature it is identical with the ones, researched in items *12.2* and *12.3, Chapter 12*.

By analogy with the systems with small number of degrees of freedom, we are going to assume that the motion is harmonic:

$$\{u\}=\{U\}\sin(\omega t+\varphi), \tag{13.2}$$

where:

$\{U\}$ is *amplitude displacements vector*.
Let us take into consideration that:

$$\{\ddot{u}\}=-\omega^2\{u\}=-\omega^2\{U\}\sin(\omega t+\varphi) \tag{13.3}$$

and from eq. (13.1) we obtain:

$$-\omega^2[m]\{u\}+[k]\{u\}=0 \tag{13.4}$$

or

$$\left[-\omega^2[m]+[k]\right]\{u\}=0. \tag{13.5}$$

In terms of to obtain non-trivial solution, it's nessecery:

$$\det \left\| [k] - \omega^2 [m] \right\| = 0. \qquad (13.6)$$

The determinant has dimensions n/n, and we have n numbers, which are roots of (13.6).

The natural frequencies are arranged in ascending order, as vector components as:

$$\{\omega\}^T = \{\omega_1 \omega_2 \omega_3 ... \omega_n\}. \qquad (13.7)$$

Each natural frequency ω_i corresponds to a *modal vector*.

The motion of the system could be expressed by the modal vectors, multiplied by corresponding coefficients λ_i. We could assume these coefficients as weight multipliers, or coefficients used for modal decomposition of the motion.

In the dynamic analysis we use mass or unit normalization of the modes. In the first case, one of the masses is assumed as referent, i.e.:

$$\overline{m}_i = C \qquad \text{or} \qquad (13.8)$$

$$\frac{m_i}{\overline{m}_i} = 1, \qquad (13.9)$$

and the other masses we express as:

$$\overline{m}_j = \frac{m_j}{\overline{m}_i}. \qquad (13.10)$$

Then, the system (13.5), modified as:

$$\left[-\omega^2 [\overline{m}] + [k] \right] \{u\} = 0 \qquad (13.11)$$

we solve n times, to obtain n modes of vibration.

If we assume that, in the direction of one of the degrees of freedom the displacement is unit, i.e. $u_k = 1$ or $u_1 = 1$, from (13.11) we could obtain the other components u_i of the corresponding modal vector.

13.2 Mass matrices

13.2.1 Mass matrix of beam finite element

The coefficients of the stiffness matrix of beam finite element we could obtain from the expression of the work of the internal and external forces, applied consecutively for each degree of freedom. In this way, for instance, for unit rotation of node i, corresponding to k_{33} from eq. (8.9), we obtain:

$$\bar{k}_{33} \times 1 = -\int_0^l A\rho\omega^2 \phi_3(x)\phi_3(x)dx + EI \int_0^l \left(\phi_3''(x)\right)^2 dx \qquad (13.12)$$

where A is the cross section of the element,
  ρ - volume density,
  ω - natural frequency, and
  $\phi_3(x)$ is shape function, related to $\varphi_i = 1$, and given by eq. (8.2).

After integration, we obtain:

$$\bar{k}_{33} = \frac{4EI}{l} - \frac{A\rho\omega^2 l^3}{105} = k_{33} - \frac{A\rho\omega^2 l^3}{105}.$$

Here $\dfrac{A\rho l^3}{105}$ represents the coefficient m_{33} of the mass matrix. We could treat it as a correction term, through which the inertial capacity of the element is taken into account.

Now we are going to express the mass matrix of beam finite element as:

$$[m] = \frac{A\rho l}{420} \begin{bmatrix} 140 & 0 & 0 & 70 & 0 & 0 \\ 0 & 156 & 22l & 0 & 54 & -13l \\ 0 & 22l & 4l^2 & 0 & 13l & -3l^2 \\ 70 & 0 & 0 & 140 & 0 & 0 \\ 0 & 54 & 13l & 0 & 156 & -22l \\ 0 & -13l & -3l^2 & 0 & -22l & 4l^2 \end{bmatrix}. \quad (13.13)$$

13.3 Evaluation of the generalized coordinates by modes

Let us consider a system with concentrated masses as shown in *Figure 13.1*. In *Figure 13.2* graphically are illustrated the displacements of the mass points, corresponding to the individual modes and the latest chart of the cited figure illustrates a superposition of these modes, i.e. multiplied by their corresponding coefficients λ_i or *modal amplitudes* Y_i.

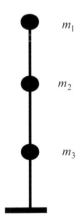

Figure 13.1: System with concentrated masses

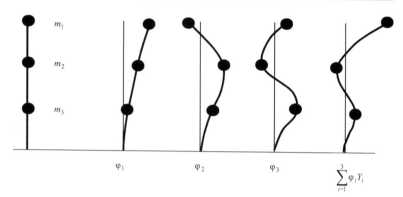

Figure 13.2: Displacements of mass points, corresponding to the modes and one possible superposition

Let us assume that, there is a similar model, but composed by m concentrated masses. The displacement of each mass, for instance i-th, from the activation of frequency ω_n could be expressed as a product of i-th component of the n-th modal vector and n-th modal amplitude:

$$u_n^i = \varphi_n^i Y_n,$$ (13.14)

where: φ_n^i is i-th component of the n-th modal vector, and Y_n —the *modal amplitude* or *generalized coordinate*, corresponding to n-th modal vector. In this case the total displacement of i-th mass is:

$$u^i = \sum_{n=1}^{m} u_n^i = \sum_{n=1}^{m} \varphi_n^i Y_n,$$ (13.15)

and for the entire system we have:

$$\mathbf{u} = \varphi \mathbf{Y}.$$ (13.16)

The matrix φ is identical with the matrix of modal vectors $[\Phi]$.

13.4 Dynamic response of MDOF system, using the Duhamel integral

The total responce of a MDOF system with n dynamic degrees of freedom could be expressed through a system of n equations. Each of these equations, (for instance i-th equations), we express as:

$$u_i'(t) = \frac{1}{m_i \omega_i} \int_0^t f(\bar{t})_i \sin \omega_i (t - \bar{t}) d\bar{t} + \sum_{j=1}^{n-1} \frac{\delta_{ij}}{m_j \omega_j} \int_0^t f(\bar{t})_j \sin \omega_j (t - \bar{t}) d\bar{t}$$

(13.17)

where: $u_i'(t)$ is the total displacement of mass i at time t,

m_i and ω_i are respectively the i-th mass, i.e. concentrated in node i and i-th natural frequency;

m_j and ω_j are respectively the j-th mass, i.e. concentrated in node j and j-th natural frequency, where is valid that $j \neq i$;

δ_{ij} is a coefficient, which value is the displacement of node i due to unit displacement of node j.

With very few exceptions, integrals (13.17) could be solved numerically. The time axis is discretized into small intervals, in a way that, in each one, for instance i-th, the load could be expressed as constant, with intensity $f(\bar{t}^i)$.

Chapter 14

Introduction to seismic mechanics. Spectrum Method. The Finite elements method in the seismic response of structures. Direct integration of the equations of motion.

14.1 Introduction

In the dynamic analysis of structures due to seismic activity we are interested only in the maximum effects and the maximum reactions. Answer of this question we could obtain through two methods. One of these methods is called *spectrum method (spectrum analysis)*. This method is based on decomposition of the seismic response to modes of vibration. One of the variations of the spectrum analysis is associated with the so-called *method of equivalent static forces*. The computational technology of this method is easily applicable and widely used in the design practice.

Another method, called *time history method*, gives us the answer of the question—what is the response, the reaction of the structure in each moment of time. This method is based on the direct integration of the equations of motion and it could authentically take into account both, the material and the geometrical non-linearity of the structure.

14.2   Seismicity and seismic waves

The powerful earthquakes lead to catastrophic consequences. That is why the research of their: nature, character and formation probability has a great importance. There are numerous existing theories, related to the facts around earthquakes formation. Each one of these theories answers some of the important questions, but the problem of the prediction of the initial moment of happening of an earthquake is still unresolved until now. In 1858, the French geologist and seismologist Antonio Snider-Pellegrini published a book, where he presented the concept of tectonic-plate structure of the Earth's crust. Based on it, in 1906 the American scientist H. F. Reid formulates a theory of earthquakes formation, called *the elastic-rebound theory*. The introduced by him, so-called mechanism of elastic reverberation, satisfactorily explains: the types of researched earthquakes, their intensity, and the virtual motion of the earth's surface.

Basically, the explanation is that an earthquake occurs due to rapture in the earth's structure. The location of this rapture is called *focus* or *hypocenter*, and its projection onto the earth's surface – *epicenter*. On the basis of the hypocenter's depth we distinguish: deep, mid-deep, and shallow or surface raptures, i.e. earthquakes. They are often quite different by their character. Due to the rapture are formed waves, called *seismic waves*. Their motion starts at the earthquake's focus, *see Figure 14.2.*

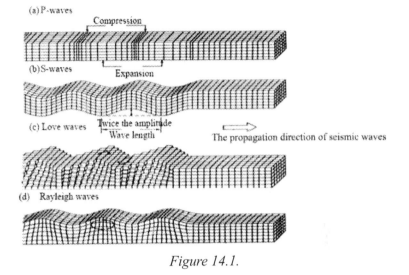

(a) P-waves

Compression

Expansion

(b) S-waves

(c) Love waves

Twice the amplitude

Wave length

The propagation direction of seismic waves

(d) Rayleigh waves

Figure 14.1.

We distinguish the following types of seismic waves:

- *P waves (primary waves);*
- *S waves (secondary waves);*
- *Love waves;*
- *Rayleigh waves.*

The motion of the material particles in the first type is in the direction of wave's propagation, as at certain moment at specific points there are (we observe) normal, i.e. compression or tension, stresses. These waves spread out with the highest speed. It is in the range of 4-8 km/s. The second type, called also transverse waves, is characterized with displacements of the material particles—transverse to the direction of the wave propagation. They spread out with a speed range of 1.8-5 km/s. When these waves are close to the earth's surface, third and forth type of seismic waves is observed, see *Figure 14.1.*

The popular *Richter scale* is based on a decimal logarithm of the maximum displacement of the surface, corrected to 100 *km* distance. It expresses as:

$$M = \log_{10} \overline{u} \,, \tag{14.1}$$

where $\overline{u}$ is the already mentioned maximum displacement of the surface.

The released energy is computed by the formulae:

$$\log E = 11.8 + 1.5M \,, \tag{14.2}$$

where M denotes the magnitude.

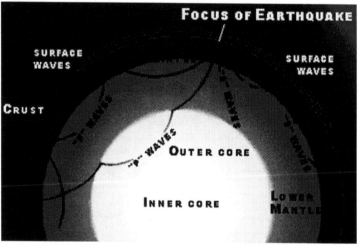

Figure 14.2.

14.3   The idea of the Spectrum method

The idea of the Spectrum method has been introduced and developed by Maurice A. Biot between 1932–1942. It is based on the so-called *elastic spectrum,* containing graphs of the maximum displacements, velocities, accelerations or other quantities of system with one degree of freedom, in the presence of viscose damping. They are obtained from the acceleration effect, applied at the base of the system, and they are expressed as a function of its natural frequency or period. Once available, they could be used for obtaining the inertial forces at the points with concentrated masses. These forces are statically equivalent to the dynamic forces and could be used for calculation of the structural response, corresponding to the modes.

We have already mentioned that this method is based on decomposition of the response by modes of vibration and often is called *linear spectrum method*. The presented method is based on the response (the displacement) of a system with one degree of freedom, expressed as:

$$u(t) = \frac{1}{m\omega} \int_0^t f(\overline{\tau}) \sin \omega (t - \overline{\tau}) d\overline{\tau}, \qquad (14.3)$$

and the total displacement, in the presence of initial displacement and velocity we express as:

$$u'(t) = \frac{\dot{u}(0) + u(0)\xi}{\omega} \sin(\omega t) + u(0)\cos(\omega t) + \frac{1}{m\omega} \int_0^t f(\overline{\tau}) \sin \omega (t - \overline{\tau}) d\overline{\tau}. \qquad (14.4)$$

In a case of structural damping eq.(14.4) we have expressed as:

$$u'(t) = \frac{\dot{u}(0)}{\omega} \sin(\omega t) + u(0)\cos(\omega t) + \frac{1}{m\omega_D} \int_0^t f(\overline{\tau}) \sin \omega_D (t - \overline{\tau}) \exp - \xi\omega (t - \overline{\tau}) d\overline{\tau}, \qquad (14.5)$$

where ω_D is damped frequency. Let us assume now that the initial displacement and velocity are missing, and the external action upon the mass is due to the acceleration at the base of massless counliliver, on which the mass m is hanging. This is illustrated in *Figure 14.3*.

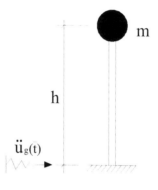

Figure 14.3

If we substitute in eq.(14.3) the function $f(\bar{t})$ with $m\ddot{u}_g(\bar{t})$, where $\ddot{u}_g(\bar{t})$ is the acceleration of the base, we obtain:

$$u(t) = \frac{1}{\omega} \int_0^t \ddot{u}_g(\bar{t}) \sin \omega (t - \bar{t}) d\bar{t}, \qquad (14.6)$$

valid in a case of absence of damping and

$$u(t) = \frac{1}{\omega_D} \int_0^t \ddot{u}_g(\bar{t}) \sin \omega_D (t - \bar{t}) \exp(-\xi\omega(t - \bar{t})) d\bar{t} \qquad (14.7)$$

in a case of damping. Eqs. (14.6) and (14.7) express the relation between the displacement of the mass and the acceleration of the base. The analysis of these relations suggests that: if we know the function of the ground acceleration, we could obtain the displacement of the mass at moment t, if its frequency and the coefficient ξ are known. From the displacement we could obtain the velocity and acceleration at moment t:

$$\dot{u}(t) = \int_0^t \ddot{u}_g(\overline{t})\cos\omega_D(t-\overline{t})\exp-\xi\omega(t-\overline{t})d\overline{t} -$$

$$-\frac{\xi\omega}{\omega_D}\int_0^t \ddot{u}_g(\overline{t})\sin\omega_D(t-\overline{t})\exp-\xi\omega(t-\overline{t})d\overline{t}$$

and (14.8)

$$\ddot{u}(t) = \omega_D\left(\xi^2\left(\frac{\omega}{\omega_D}\right)^2 - 1\right)\int_0^t \ddot{u}_g(\overline{t})\sin\omega_D(t-\overline{t})\exp-\xi\omega(t-\overline{t})d\overline{t} -$$

$$-2\omega\xi\int_0^t \ddot{u}_g(\overline{t})\cos\omega_D(t-\overline{t})\exp-\xi\omega(t-\overline{t})d\overline{t}$$

.

(14.9)

14.4   Application of the Spectrum method

For each dynamic analysis it is necessary the frequencies or the periods and modes of vibration to be preliminary known. They are used as a basis for successive computations.

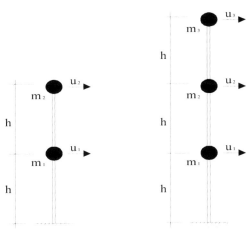

Figure 14.4

The already mentioned equivalent forces are computational storey seismic forces, corresponding to a specific mode of vibration. They could be obtained through the formulae:

$$E_{ik} = CRk_c\beta_i\eta_{ik}Q_k,$$ (14.10)

where: E_{ik} is a computational storey seismic force, acting at mass point (storey level) k, corresponding to mode i;

C - coefficient of importance of the building or the construction,

R - coefficient of the reaction of the structure;

k_c - seismic coefficient of the site, where the building is located. This coefficient is the ratio of the maximum acceleration of the earth's surface to the gravity acceleration, i.e. $k_c = a_{max}^g / g$, taken from seismic map.

β_i - dynamic coefficient, corresponding to $i–th$ mode. It can be taken from graphs, see *Figure 14.5,* or could be obtained from the following relations:

$$0.8 \le \beta_i = \frac{0.9}{T_i} \le 2.5 \text{ for soils group A and B};$$ (14.11)

$$0.8 \le \beta_i = \frac{1.2}{T_i} \le 2.5 \text{ for soils group C};$$ (14.12)

$$1.0 \le \beta_i = \frac{1.6}{T_i} \le 2.5 \text{ for soils group D}.$$ (14.13)

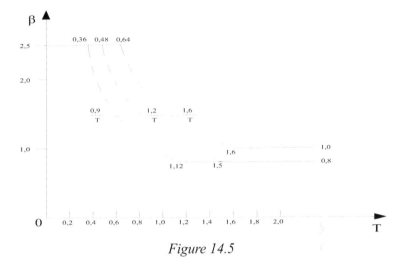

Figure 14.5

This coefficient depends on the periods of vibration and on the soils group.

η_{ik} - coefficient of distribution of the computational seismic forces to modes, obtained as:

$$\eta_{ik} = X_{ik} \frac{\sum_{j=1}^{n} X_{ij} Q_j}{\sum_{j=1}^{n} X_{ij}^2 Q_j}. \qquad (14.14)$$

In the above relation X_{ik} or X_{ij} denotes: modal coordinates (normalized modal displacements) for mass k and j, corresponding to mode i. Here n is number of the modes.

Q_k - storey weight, concentrated at the point k.

In eq. (14.14) the multiplier behind X_{ik} could be interpreted as *modal participation factor (coefficient)*. If we multiply the dynamic coefficient β_i by k_c, R and g we will obtain the spectral relation $S_a - T_i$. This spectral relation we could express also as $S_a - \omega_i$. Then, to obtain the computational storey seismic forces, we could use:

$$E_{ik} = CS_a\left(T_i\right)_i \eta_{ik} m_k \tag{14.15}$$

or

$$E_{ik} = CS_a\left(\omega_i\right)_i \eta_{ik} m_k , \tag{14.16}$$

where $S_a\left(T_i\right) = Rk_c\beta_i\left(T_i\right)g$ and $S_a\left(\omega_i\right) = Rk_c\beta_i\left(\omega_i\right)g$.

In *Eurocode 8* the computational elastic spectrum of accelerations is defined as a function of the period T with three of its characteristic points T_B, T_C and T_D, *Figure 14.6*. They depend on the type of the soil and possess the following meaning:

T_B and T_C - the left and right limits of the constant branch;

T_D - value of the period, defining the beginning of constant response range.

The relations, constructing the curve $S_a\left(T\right)$ are:

$$S_a\left(T\right) = a_{gd}S\left[1 + \frac{T}{T_B}\left(2,5\eta - 1\right)\right], \qquad \text{for } 0 \leq T \leq T_B$$

$$S_a\left(T\right) = a_{gd}S2,5\eta, \qquad \text{for } T_B \leq T \leq T_C$$

$$S_a\left(T\right) = a_{gd}S2,5\eta\left(\frac{T_C}{T}\right), \qquad \text{for } T_C \leq T \leq T_D$$

$$S_a\left(T\right)=a_{gd}S2,5\eta\left(\frac{T_cT_D}{T^2}\right), \qquad \text{for } T_D \leq T \leq 4s,$$

where: $S_a\left(T\right)$ is the elastic spectrum of accelerations and could be expressed also with $S_e\left(T\right)$; T - period of vibration for equivalent linear SDOF; a_{gd} - design acceleration of the ground for soil—type A. It is obtained from $a_{gd} = \gamma a_{gR}$. Here γ is coefficient of importance. S is soil factor; η—the correction factor.

In *Figure 14.6* the shape of elastic spectrum of accelerations is shown.

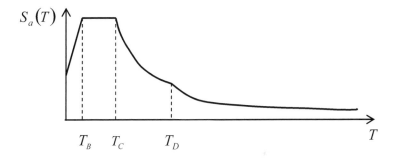

Figure 14.6. Elastic spectrum of accelerations.

Once obtained through formulae (14.10), for mode i, the seismic forces must be applied as equivalent static forces, and in this way we could obtain the stresses and internal forces of the structure, corresponding to mode i. The total stresses and internal forces we obtain through the so-called combination of modal responses. For this purpose we use several relations. The most frequently used is:

$$R = \sqrt{\sum_{i=1}^{n} R_i^2}, \qquad (14.17)$$

153

where R_i is a given quantity, computed for *i-th* mode of vibration. This method is called *Square-Root-of-Sum-of-Squares (SRSS) method*. It gives satisfactory results in regular in plan and altitude structures, where similar by value frequencies are missing. Another, commonly used method, is the *Complete Quadratic Combination (CQC) method*

$$R = \sqrt{\sum_{i=1}^{n}\sum_{j=1}^{n}\rho_{ij}R_iR_j} , \qquad (14.18)$$

where R_i and R_j denote the values of given quantities, computed respectively for *i-th* and *j-th* modes, and ρ_{ij} are so-called coefficients of modes interaction.

The number of used in the seismic analysis modes say n, affects the accuracy of the computational results. A verification of the accuracy could be performed through the formulae:

$$\varsigma_n = \frac{\sum_{i=1}^{n}\bar{M}_i}{M_{total}} \le 1, \qquad (14.19)$$

where: ς_n is the effective modal mass index;

$\sum_{i=1}^{n}\bar{M}_i$ - sum of the effective modal masses for all n modes, used in the analysis;

M_{total} - total construction's mass.

It is required this index to be higher than 95% in two-dimensional and 90% in three-dimensional computational models.

In addition, it is required to be verified whether the effective modal masses, higher in value than 5% of the total mass, have been registered.

If the sufficiency verification of the registered modes of vibration has not been satisfied, then the number of the modes could be increased, or so-called *static correction* could be used.

What follows next is: combination by coordinate directions. It is performed by the *SRSS (Square-Root-of-Sum-of-Squares) method,* expresses as:

$$N_j = \sqrt{\left(N_j^x\right)^2 + \left(N_j^y\right)^2},$$

where N_j is given quantity in section j; N_j^x is the same quantity in section j, obtained from the seismic forces, applied in x; N_j^y is the same quantity in section j, obtained from the seismic forces, applied in y.

Other ways of combination by coordinate directions could be used, as well. One of them is based on the expressions:

$$N_j = N_j^x \oplus 0.3 N_j^y$$

$$N_j = 0.3 N_j^x \oplus N_j^y$$

where only the horizontal seismic forces are used, and

$$N_j = N_j^x \oplus 0.3 N_j^y \oplus 0.3 N_j^z$$

$$N_j = 0.3 N_j^x \oplus N_j^y \oplus 0.3 N_j^z$$

$$N_j = 0.3 N_j^x \oplus 0.3 N_j^y \oplus N_j^z$$

where also the vertical components of the seismic forces are used.

The real displacements could be obtained through the elastic displacements, using R or the so-called *behavior factor.*

14.5 Application of the FEM in the Spectrum method

This application we are going to systematize in an algorithm.

- *Generation of the computational model. Choice of the mass distribution and degrees of freedom. This stage is highly important for the accuracy of the results;*
- *Performing of a modal analysis in terms to obtain the frequencies, and the corresponding modes of vibration;*
- *Introducing or choosing the spectrum, the coefficients, and the quantities necessary in terms to perform the spectrum analysis;*
- *Combining the results by a selected methods;*
- *Combining by coordinate directions;*
- *Interpreting and using the results.*

14.6 Method of direct integration of the equations of motion

The method of direct integration is based on discretization of the time axis, and performance of numerical integration. This method creates opportunity for highly precise analyses of complex structures, taking into account their material and geometrical non-linearity. This method registers the real displacements, strains, and other quantities in each specific moment t, taking into consideration the above mentioned non-linearities. The actual distribution of the dessipativity and the developed plasticity, strictly individual for each specific structure, lead to different displacements at its points. This kind of displacements we could obtain more precisely, i.e. more accurately, through the methods of direct integration of the equations of motion, used in the technology of the Finite element method.

References

[1]   Banko B.; *Theory of elasticity, stability and dynamics of structures*, UACG, (*in Bulgarian*), 2006

[2]   Bathe K, and Wilson E.; *Numerical Methods in Finite Element Analysis*. Prentice-Hall, 1976

[3]   Chopra Anil.; *Dynamics of Structures*. Prentice Hall, 2006

[4]   Clough R., J. Penzie.; *Dynamics of Structures*. Mcgraw-Hill College, 1975

[5]   Fenner R. Finite.; *Element Methods for Engineers*. Imperial College Press, Second reprint, 1997

[6]   Kazakov K.; *The Finite element method in structural analysis*. Academic publishing house "Marin Drinov", BAS, Sofia, 2009

[7]   Kazakov K.; *Theory of elasticity, stability and dynamics of structures*, Academic publishing house "Marin Drinov", BAS, Sofia, 2010

[8]   Muskhelishvili N. *Some basic problems of the mathematical theory of elasticity*. Groningen, P. Noordhoff, 1953

[9]   Timoshenko S. *Theory of Elasticity*. New York, McGraw-Hill, 1934

[10] Timoshenko St., James Gere. *Theory of Elastic Stability*. McGraw-Hill Book Company, 1st Ed., 1936

[11] Zienkiewicz O., R. Taylor, J Zhu. *The Finite Element Method: Its Basis and Fundamentals*, McGraw-Hill, 1967